In his book, *And Then the End Will Come*, Doug Cobb takes a humble and holistic approach to better understanding what the Bible teaches concerning the return of Christ. I love that this book doesn't get lost in the eschatological weeds and that it doesn't just convey information, but it explores the implications of how we must live, love, and lead as the end draws near."

Kyle Idleman, senior pastor, Southeast Christian Church, author, *not a fan*, *AHA*, and *Grace Is Greater*

"I've known Doug Cobb for thirty years. He is the real deal. You will be blessed and encouraged by sitting at Doug's feet, and his thoroughly researched and biblical book will fill you with hope that 'doesn't disappoint.'"

Paul Miller, author, *A Praying Life* and *J-Curve*

"*And Then the End Will Come* is so needed for times like these. This biblically based, easy-to-follow study of the second coming deepens confidence in the truth of God's Word, inspires hope in desperate times, motivates us to holy living, and reignites the fires of evangelism. Be encouraged by it while you 'wait for the blessed hope—the glorious appearing of our great God and Savior, Jesus Christ.'"

Bob Russell, founder, Bob Russell Ministries

"This book is power packed, fast paced, solid, and thorough. It's worth the read! But as you delve in, don't seek to be merely informed. Doug is extending an invitation for all of us to join in the greatest faith adventure known to humankind."

Eric Watt, president, Reaching Unreached Nations

"Christians believe Jesus is coming back, but we rarely explore or seek to understand it. In this book, Doug Cobb guides us with biblical richness to see that the Bible has much to say to prepare us for this great day."

John Rinehart, author, *Gospel Patrons*

"Regardless of your take on biblical prophecy, there is one sure promise of Jesus: he will return. As Doug Cobb explains in *And Then the End Will Come*, some of us believe that we are very close to seeing the gospel proclaimed everywhere. Your heart will be lifted as you read Doug's new book."

Paul Eshleman, founder, The Jesus Film Project and founding director, Finishing the Task

"*And Then The End Will Come* reveals that The End is at hand. Through Doug Cobb's Finishing Fund, and now this book, he has been a trailblazer in the work of making disciples in foreign lands. After 2,000-plus years, Jesus command for us to 'make disciples of all nations' is almost complete. Doug's message for the world is: People get ready, Jesus is coming."

Rusty George, senior pastor Real Life Church
and author of *After Amen*

"Doug Cobb's excitement about completing the Great Commission is infectious. With wit and wisdom, he shares the Christo-centric way to finishing the task in this decade. Moreover, from Isaiah and Daniel through 2 Peter and Revelation, Doug reveals the Biblical path to the coming Christ. Rest assured, if you are a Christ-follower, you will be inspired by the fellow-laborers working to bring about His Kingdom Come. Read *And Then The End Will Come*, and you will be encouraged."

Jarrett Stephens, senior pastor Champion Forest
and author of *The Always God*

Douglas Cobb

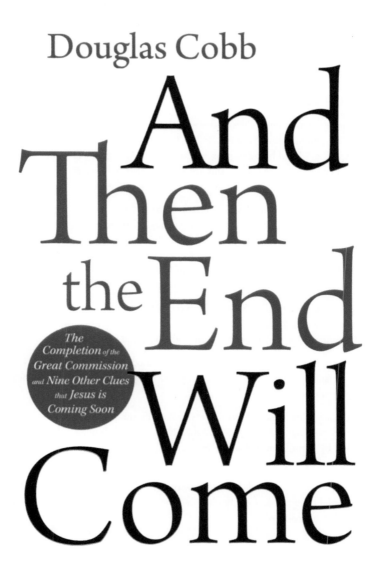

And Then the End Will Come

The Completion *of the* Great Commission *and* Nine Other Clues *that* Jesus is Coming Soon

Forward by Bob Shank

DEEPWATER BOOKS

Cover design by Micah Kandros
Interior design by PerfecType, Nashville, TN
Edited by Marissa Wold Uhrina
ISBN 978-0-9994671-4-5
Printed in the United States of America

To Paul Eshleman,
who invited me into the adventure of a lifetime.

ACKNOWLEDGMENTS

Gena, my beautiful wife: thank you for always supporting my adventures. I am so thankful that you love God, love His Word, and love me!

Kyle Idleman, Bob Russell, Tom and Karen Harper, Bob Shank, Don Gates, Doug Michael, John Rinehart, and Gena Cobb: thank you for reviewing the manuscript, for your helpful suggestions, and most of all for your encouragement.

Tom Harper: thanks for your encouragement and assistance and for taking me under your wing.

My brothers and sisters in Word by Word: thank you for allowing me to teach the book to you and for your questions and suggestions. You have no idea how much that helped. I love living life with you.

My fellow elders at Southeast Christian: the finest group of men I've ever been associated with.

My partners in the Finishing Fund: thank you for your generosity and for your confidence in me.

Mike Constanz, Lisa Pak, Dan Hitzhusen, Dante and Katya Tamez, Cindy Deibert, and Lara Heneveld of Finishing the Task:

ACKNOWLEDGMENTS

thanks for all of your hard work and help as we work toward the day when there are "disciples in every nation."

Len Moisan: thanks for modeling what a great Bible teacher looks like.

David Reagan and Lamb & Lion Ministries: thank you for many years of great teaching on prophecy and the last days.

Miss Merriman and Mrs. Bendt: thanks for doing your best to teach me how to write.

CONTENTS

CONTENTS

FOREWORD

In an earlier era—when daily newspapers were the primary way to communicate significant reports to a mass audience—editors used an insider term for front-page, above-the-fold headlines: "Second Coming Type."

The premise was simple: a certain font size was reserved for only the most earth-shaking, unprecedented occasions. The attack on Pearl Harbor, the assassination of a president, a stock market crash—these were historic events that, like the return of Jesus, required striking emphasis, demanding the full focus of the reader.

In the first century, the apostle Peter foresaw the decline of interest in the return of the Lord Jesus Christ: "Where is this 'coming' he promised? Ever since our ancestors died, everything goes on as it has from the beginning of creation" (2 Pet. 3:4).

Based on Peter's prophetic projection, it's no surprise that today's major news purveyors have no interest in covering current trends and events that point toward an apocalyptic culmination of history. Biblical prophecy has been consigned to the realm of fables and superstition.

But for those whose faith is in Jesus and confidence is in the Scriptures, this should be a time of astounding anticipation concerning the unfolding fulfillment of God's promises. Yet many today are unaware or confused about the milestones that mark the journey from today's growing darkness to the light of the coming kingdom.

Do your own research: find Christians who frequent Bible studies and who attend churches where the Scriptures are faithfully taught, and ask them to summarize the significant global events that signal the soon coming of That Day. Give them a pad of paper; ask them to sketch the prophecies and promises that chart the course to the moment when God will make all things new, and anticipate an embarrassed silence to follow.

In *And Then the End Will Come*, Doug Cobb has taken on the assignment of enlightening people who love God and hope for heaven about the biblical truths concerning that which is unfolding around us today.

This is not an academic treatise; instead, Doug will draw you from the ranks of the uninformed, passively watching what unfolds before them, into the camp of proactive followers of Jesus who are influencing the timeline of God's history.

Every thoughtful Christian must rise above the demands of each day to ask the overarching question: What should be the ultimate focus of my life, from here to heaven? The next-to-last verse of Revelation—as John quotes the Lord Jesus himself—summarizes the ultimate: "He who testifies to these things says, 'Yes, I am coming soon.' Amen. Come, Lord Jesus" (Rev. 22:20).

He is coming soon. The mission left for us—for you, for me—to complete before that promise can be realized is the discovery waiting for you in the pages of this book. Beyond the biblical truths that led to your salvation in Jesus Christ, this may be the most important message for you to understand and engage with for the rest of your lifetime. I invite you to thoughtfully read the twelve chapters that follow and come to your own conclusion. I think you'll be inspired and enlightened.

Bob Shank

Founder, The Master's Program

INTRODUCTION

In the book of Habakkuk, Chapter 1, the LORD speaks to the prophet and says,

> Look at the nations and watch—
> and be utterly amazed.
> For I am going to do something in your days
> that you would not believe,
> even if you were told. (Hab. 1:5)

This prophecy was originally a warning: God was raising up the Babylonians to bring judgment and destruction on Judah—something they did not believe could happen, even though God had told them it would.

But these words are as relevant to us today as they were to those people long ago. God is doing utterly amazing—even unbelievable—things in our day, working through his people to complete Jesus' Great Commission: "go and make disciples of all nations" (Matt. 28:19). By God's grace, the worldwide church is only a few years away from the finish line of the two-thousand-year Great Commission race. We live in the most momentous time since Jesus walked the earth.

1

Sadly, though, the church in the West is largely unaware of these things. Most believers don't know that the completion of the Great Commission is at hand. Few understand that Jesus directly linked his second coming to that event, saying in Matthew 24:14, "This gospel of the kingdom will be preached in the whole world as a testimony to all nations, *and then the end will come*." What's more, most have not been exposed to a number of other biblical prophecies that also signal Jesus' return in the near future. As a result, we are discouraged by the chaos and decline we see around us, rather than seeing those things as necessary precursors to the wonderful things soon to come.

If it's true that Jesus' return is imminent, we should be joyful and excited, even in the midst of the growing craziness we see around us in the world, knowing that our "blessed hope" is close at hand. And we should be all the more serious about preparing ourselves for his return, because time is short. Instead, we're a lot like the church at Sardis described in Revelation 3: asleep and unaware of the amazing things happening in our day. Jesus tells that church, "If you do not wake up, I will come like a thief, and you will not know at what time I will come to you" (Rev. 3:3).

I've written this book to inform you about the worldwide movement that is finishing the Great Commission; to acquaint you with other biblical clues that confirm the promise of Matthew 24:14; to encourage you to get ready for the coming Day of God; and to fill you with joy about the things God has prepared for us in the age to come—things so astounding that the Bible says no one can even imagine how fantastic they will be. I hope it will be a blessing and that it will awaken you to the amazing things that God is doing in our day.

. . .

I became interested in this subject though my involvement with Finishing the Task, an organization created by my mentor, Paul Eshleman, to mobilize the worldwide church to complete the Great Commission. Through FTT I learned that there is a real chance that our generation can complete that task. God's Spirit is at work in a powerful way around the world today, bringing in a great harvest of new believers from places where Jesus' name has never before been heard. Hundreds of people groups—the Bible calls them "nations"—are hearing the gospel for the first time every year.

My involvement with FTT led my wife, Gena, and me to begin funding indigenous missionaries to go to people groups in India, Nepal, and Nigeria who had never heard the gospel. We were privileged to hear amazing stories of the first known believers in history from among these groups. Those experiences led me to launch the Finishing Fund, a partnership of generous Christians who are giving together to finish this task. As of December 2020, the partners of the Fund have helped send the gospel to more than 450 people groups who had never heard it before. By God's grace, our mission is to see every people group on earth engaged with the gospel by the end of 2022.

It was also through FTT that I became aware of the kingdom significance of finishing the task—that according to Matthew 24:14 its completion will open the door for Jesus' return and the end of the age. For most of history, the Great Commission finish line—and thus his return—has been far in the future. But if we're very close to finishing today, could it be that we are also very close to his return? I think we are.

Understanding the implications of Matthew 24:14 led me to begin seeking other biblical evidence that the return of Christ might be near. That search resulted in clues presented in this book: the regathering of the nation of Israel, the prophecies of Daniel 12 and Hosea 5 and 6, the approaching end of six thousand years of biblical history, the acceleration of travel and knowledge, the condition of the church and culture today, and others. Each of these, I believe, is a sign that we are living in the very last days. I hope you'll read on to see if you agree.

• • •

I've done my best to make this book accessible to anyone who has interest in this subject: laypeople, Bible teachers, pastors, even curious skeptics. This is a book about what the Bible says regarding the second coming, so I quote a lot of Scripture in it. Some of the math gets a little dense in chapters 5 and 6, but I've tried to make that as simple as possible.

I believe in a pre-tribulation rapture and a literal thousand-year, or millennial, reign of Christ on the earth, and those opinions show up in this book. I understand that many believers hold different views about those events. Even if you see things differently, I think you'll find this book worthwhile. For the most part, the clues are relevant no matter what eschatological position you take.

I am not a prophet. Despite my best efforts to understand and explain these prophecies, I'm aware that my conclusions could be wrong. Having said that, though, Isaiah 46:10 tells us we have a God who makes "known the end from the beginning, from ancient times, what is still to come." He revealed to Daniel the precise time of Jesus' first coming and provided abundant prophecies that unmistakably identify Jesus of Nazareth as the promised Messiah. It makes sense to me that he would likewise provide clues about the timing of Jesus' second coming and that he might actually have revealed it just as precisely.

Here's the point: I believe Jesus is coming back in my expected lifetime—and probably yours as well. That means we may have the privilege of experiencing some amazing things that believers have been looking forward to for thousands of years. But it also means that the Bible's admonitions to "live holy and godly lives as [we] look forward to the day of God" (2 Pet. 3:11–12) apply with special importance to us. If we are privileged to see Christ's return, we want to be ready.

Some generation is going to experience the blessing of witnessing the return of Christ. Those believers will not suffer death but will transition directly from life in this world into eternal life— what the Bible calls "the life that is truly life" (1 Tim. 6:19). They will be raised up to join him and will from that point on live with him forever. Could ours be the generation privileged to experience those things? I think we could. And wouldn't that be awesome?

So let's dive in. Because he is coming back. And it's going to be soon!

Unveiling
the
Promise

1

He *Is* Coming Back

One thing is certain: Jesus *is* coming back. The message of this book is that he's coming soon. But even if I'm wrong about that, we can be confident that one day he will return.

How can we be sure? Because from beginning to end, the Bible promises that Jesus will return to rule over the earth forever from the throne of his ancestor David.

There are hundreds of passages in the Old and New Testaments that prophesy the return of Christ. Herbert Lockyear, in his book *All the Messianic Prophecies of the Bible*, says that the second coming is mentioned 318 times in the New Testament.[1] And Alfred Edersheim's classic book *The Life and Time of Jesus the Messiah* documents 456 Old Testament passages that were considered messianic prophecies by Jewish scholars prior to the coming of Christ[2]—some related to the first coming, some to the second, and some to both.

I often remind my Sunday school classmates that God's promises—and after all, what are prophecies but promises?—are the most real thing we know. If God has promised something, it will certainly occur. There is more chance of the chair I'm sitting on dissolving into thin air and dumping me on the floor than there is of even one of God's promises not coming true.

The Bible says that God's "very great and precious promises" are rooted in "his own glory and goodness" (2 Pet. 1:3–4). Glory means that he is so great, so powerful, so fully in control that nothing and no one can deter him from doing what he wants to do. As he says in Isaiah 46:10, "My purpose will stand, and I will do all that I please."

If the Bible is true, there is no doubt: Jesus is coming back.

Goodness means that God's character is so flawless that he would never lie or deceive us, telling us that he will do something and then reneging on the promise. As we read in Numbers 23:19, "God is not human, that he should lie, not a human being, that he should change his mind. Does he speak, and then not act? Does he promise and not fulfill?"

So if the Bible is true, there is no doubt: Jesus *is* coming back.

Prophecies of the First Coming

Before we consider the prophecies about the second coming, let's take a minute to reflect on the amazing way God predicted the Messiah's first coming. The Old Testament contains hundreds of prophecies about Jesus' first coming, such as:

- He would be born of a virgin (Isa. 7:14).
- He would be born in Bethlehem (Mic. 5:2).
- He would live in Egypt during his childhood (Hosea 11:1).
- He would be David's descendant (Jer. 23:5–6).
- He would be a Galilean (Isa. 9:1–2).

Daniel 9 includes the famous prophecy of the seventy weeks, including the claim that "from the time the word goes out to restore and rebuild Jerusalem until the Anointed One, the ruler, comes, there will be seven 'sevens,' and sixty-two 'sevens'" (Dan. 9:25). When we consider this mysterious prophecy in chapter 5, we'll see that it predicted precisely the year of the first coming of the Messiah.

The Jewish rabbis of Jesus' day had concluded that there were three miracles that only the Messiah would be able to perform: cleansing a Jewish leper, casting out a demon that made its victim mute, and giving sight to a man born blind. While these are not strictly biblical prophecies, Jesus nevertheless explicitly fulfilled each of them; you can read the stories in Luke 5, Matthew 12, and John 9. These miracles established Jesus' claim to be the Messiah beyond a shadow of a doubt. Amazingly, it was in direct response to these proofs that the Jewish leaders turned away and hardened their hearts toward him.

The Old Testament contains numerous prophecies concerning just the events surrounding Jesus' death. For example:

- He would be betrayed by a close friend for thirty pieces of silver (Ps. 41:9, Zech. 11:12).
- His bones would not be broken (Num. 9:12).
- His clothing would be divided by casting lots (Ps. 22:18).

- He would be crucified among criminals outside the city (Isa. 53:12; Lev. 16:27).
- He would be buried in a rich man's tomb (Isa. 53:9).

Finally, the Old Testament repeatedly predicts that the Messiah would be raised from the dead. Isaiah 53:11 says, "After he has suffered, he will see the light of life and be satisfied; by his knowledge my righteous servant will justify many, and he will bear their iniquities."

These are only a handful of the Old Testament prophecies concerning the first coming of the Messiah—but they should be more than enough. The chances of all of these predictions being fulfilled in the life of one person is infinitesimally small—so miniscule that there can be no doubt that Jesus of Nazareth, in whose life they were perfectly fulfilled, is the promised Messiah.

But for our purposes the importance of these prophecies of Jesus' *first* coming is to give us confidence that the many prophecies of his *second* coming will also be fulfilled. Let's take a look at some of those.

What Did Jesus Say?

Jesus himself explicitly promised that he would return, when he told his disciples,

"My Father's house has many rooms; if that were not so, would I have told you that I am going there to prepare a place for you? And if I go and prepare a place for you, *I will come back* and take you to be with me that you also may be where I am." (John 14:1–3)

It really couldn't be clearer than that, could it? Jesus said, "I *will* come back."

In Matthew 16:27, Jesus says, "For the Son of Man *is going to come* in his Father's glory with his angels, and then he will reward each person according to what they have done." "Son of Man" is one of Jesus' favorite titles for himself, so when he says, "the Son of Man is going to come," he's speaking of his own return. And again, notice the absolute certainty of Jesus' language: "the Son of Man *is going to come.*"

In Matthew 24, Jesus urges his followers to be on the alert for his return: "Therefore keep watch, because you do not know on what day *your Lord will come.* . . . So you also must be ready, because *the Son of Man will come* at an hour when you do not expect him" (Matt. 24:42, 44). We usually read this passage as a caution about predicting *when* Jesus will return, but notice that it also confirms that he *will* come back: Jesus says, "your Lord *is* coming" and "the Son of man *is* coming."

Jesus himself explicitly promised that he would return.

At the end of Matthew 24 and in Mathew 25, Jesus used parables to describe the need to be prepared and productive while we wait for his return. Then in 25:31 he says, "*When the Son of Man comes* in his glory, and all the angels with him, he will sit on his glorious throne." Not "*If* the Son of Man comes"—*when* he comes. *When* he comes, he will sit on his throne and judge the entire earth.

Finally, the last words of Jesus recorded in Scripture, in Revelation 22:20, are, "Yes, *I am coming soon.*" In fact, Jesus repeats these words three times, and the words *come* and *coming* appear seven times in that one chapter. He clearly wants us to be confident that he *is* coming back!

The Old Testament

As we've seen, the Old Testament includes many prophecies of the Messiah's first coming. But it contains even more prophecies about his return.

Some Old Testament passages predict the return of Christ unambiguously. Daniel 7 describes Daniel's vision of

> *one like a son of man, coming* with the clouds of heaven. He approached the Ancient of Days and was led into his presence. He was given authority, glory and sovereign power; all nations and peoples of every language worshiped him. His dominion is an everlasting dominion that will not pass away, and his kingdom is one that will never be destroyed. (Dan. 7:13–14)

In this passage Daniel describes a vision of "one like a son of man" who is given an everlasting kingdom spanning the entire earth. That's the Messiah. And in the context, it's clear that his coming will take place at the end of human history, after a succession of world empires has come and gone.

One of the most vivid prophecies about the second coming is found in Zechariah 14:1–5. Many believe that this passage describes the return of Christ with his church at the end of the seven-year tribulation. When all the nations of the earth have gathered against Jerusalem, Jesus will return to defeat his enemies and establish his earthly kingdom. It concludes, "Then *the* LORD *my God will come, and all the holy ones with him*" (Zech. 14:5).

Some Old Testament prophecies conflate Jesus' first and second comings. For example, Isaiah 9:6 says, "For to us a child is born, to us a son is given," which is an apparent reference to the birth of Christ. But verse 7 continues with a prophecy of Jesus' second coming as the eternal King, saying that "of the greatness of his government and peace there will be no end" and that "*He will reign on David's throne* and over his kingdom establishing and upholding it with justice and righteousness *from that time on and forever.*"

Another example is Isaiah 61:2, which speaks of "the year of the LORD's favor"—a prophecy of Jesus' first coming—and "the day of vengeance of our God"—a reference to the time of his return—in a single verse.

Passages like these are one reason Bible prophecy can be difficult to understand. They help explain why the Jews were confused about Jesus' first coming—they weren't able to glean the prophecies about the suffering servant from the prophecies about the coming king.

For this reason, some have compared studying prophecy to viewing a mountain range. From a distance the various peaks appear to be part of one range. But as you draw closer you see that they are actually separate peaks, with valleys in between.

There are many more Old Testament prophecies about the coming of the Messiah. Some focus on the promise of a coming righteous king, a descendant of David, who will rule on David's throne forever. Others predict that he is coming as a righteous judge. Still other prophecies describe the regathering of Israel that will take place before the Messiah returns. You could easily spend months exploring everything the Word of God has to say about the second coming of the Messiah.

The New Testament

The apostles and the other New Testament authors took seriously Jesus' claims that he would return. Guided by the Holy Spirit, they wrote frequently about the second coming and the events and circumstances that would surround it.

In Acts 1, we're told that the disciples were "looking intently up into the sky" as Jesus ascended into heaven, when two angels appeared to them and asked them why they were looking up. They said, "This same Jesus, who has been taken from you into heaven, *will come back* in the same way you have seen him go into heaven" (Acts 1:11). Jesus *will* come back in the same way he departed: in the clouds.

The promise that the Lord is returning is found in almost every book in the New Testament.

The two letters to the church at Thessalonica were written because some in that church feared they had missed the rapture and were living in the tribulation. In those letters, Paul reassures them that they had not missed out and describes the circumstances that will surround Jesus' return. In 1 Thessalonians 4:16 Paul says, "For the *Lord himself will come down* from heaven, with a loud command, with the voice of the archangel and with the trumpet call of God . . ."

The idea that the Lord is returning, and returning soon, is found in almost every book in the New Testament. For example, James 5:7–8 says, "Be patient and stand firm, because the *Lord's coming is near.*" Likewise, in 1 Corinthians 11:26, when Paul teaches about the Lord's Supper, he says, "For whenever you eat this bread and drink this cup, you proclaim the Lord's death *until he comes.*"

Hebrews 9:27–28 reminds us, "Christ was sacrificed once to take away the sins of many; and *he will appear a second time*, not to bear sin, but to bring salvation to those who are waiting for him." This verse is an important reminder that Jesus' second coming will not be like his first. He came the first time not "to condemn the world, but to save the world" (John 3:17), but when he returns, it will be in power to redeem his people and judge his enemies.

And finally, the New Testament book of Revelation describes the vision God gave to the apostle John of the events of the last days, including the return of Christ. In Revelation 19:11–16 we read this amazing description of John's vision of Jesus' return:

> I saw heaven standing open and there before me was a white horse, whose rider is called Faithful and True. With justice he judges and wages war. His eyes are like blazing fire, and on his head are many crowns. He has a name written on him that no one knows but he himself. He is dressed in a robe dipped in blood, and his name is the Word of God. The armies of heaven were following him, riding on white horses and dressed in fine linen, white and clean. Coming out of his mouth is a sharp sword with which to strike down the nations. "He will rule them with an iron scepter." He treads the winepress of the fury of the wrath of God Almighty. On his robe and on his thigh he has this name written:
>
> KING OF KINGS AND LORD OF LORDS.

That this passage is describing Jesus Christ is evident from the titles it gives him: in verse 13, "The Word of God," reminiscent of John 1; and in verse 16, "KING OF KINGS AND LORD OF LORDS," echoing 1 Timothy 6:15.

Our Blessed Hope

I hope that reading these prophecies fills you with joyful anticipation. But you might have reservations. If you're younger and there are places you'd like to go and things you'd like to see; or if you're working on something—like completing a degree or building a business—that will take time to complete; or if you're waiting to get married or have children or for your children to grow up, you may find yourself hoping that Jesus will tarry for a while.

In his letter to Titus, Paul reminds us that the return of Christ is "our blessed hope." He says, "the grace of God . . . teaches us to say 'No' to ungodliness and worldly passions, and to live self-controlled, upright and godly lives in this present age, *while we wait for our blessed hope—the appearing of the glory of our great God and Savior, Jesus Christ*" (Titus 2:11–13).

Consider what the return of Christ will mean. No more death, crying, sorrow, or pain. Every tear wiped away. No more sin and so no more struggle against sin. No more curse. Hunger, poverty, disease—gone. Worldwide justice, peace, and righteousness. The personal presence of God, forever and ever, everywhere. Literally, it will be heaven on earth!

No matter how awesome your life is—or how awesome you're hoping it may become—it does not begin to compare to life in the kingdom of God. Paul says in 1 Corinthians 2:9 (NLT), "No eye has seen, no ear has heard, and no mind has imagined what God has prepared for those who love him." I can imagine some pretty amazing things, but God's Word promises that what he has in store for us far exceeds even that.

God wants us to eagerly antici- *For believers, the* pate Jesus' return. Second Peter 3:12 *return of Christ is* instructs us to "*look forward* to the *"our blessed hope."* day of God and speed its coming." In Philippians 3:20, Paul reminds us that "our citizenship is in heaven. And we *eagerly* await a Savior from there, the Lord Jesus Christ . . ." Likewise, in 2 Timothy 4:8, Paul promises a reward—a crown of glory—for "all who have *longed* for his appearing."

So if you're a follower of Jesus, I want to encourage you to look forward to his return and his kingdom. It's going to be awesome.

An Invitation

But if you don't know Jesus—if you haven't trusted him as your Lord and Savior—then his return will be a time of great grief. Today, while we wait for Jesus to return, we live in a time of abundant mercy and grace. Jesus came the first time to live the life we all should be living and die the death we all deserve. His death paid a debt that none of us could pay for ourselves. Thanks to his sacrifice, forgiveness and eternal life are free for the asking. All one has to do is acknowledge him for who he is—the Son of God and the Lord over all creation—and believe that God has raised him from the dead.

Once he returns, that door will be closed. It will be too late. The judge will have come. Revelation 6:15–17 warns that on the day Jesus returns, "the kings of the earth, the princes, the generals, the rich, the mighty, and everyone else, both slave and free, [will hide] in caves and among the rocks of the mountains" and beg them to " 'fall on us and hide us from the face of him who sits on the throne and from the wrath of the Lamb! For the great day of their wrath has come, and who can withstand it?' "

So with all my heart, I say: if you haven't received God's gift of forgiveness and eternal life through his Son Jesus Christ, make today the day. He wants to forgive you, heal you, complete you, and give you a new family and a new purpose for life. Give your life to him and join all of us who are eagerly looking for his return.

Where Is He?

Many these days are skeptical about the return of Christ. The apostle Peter addresses those doubters in chapter 3 of his second epistle:

> First, I want to remind you that in the last days there will come scoffers who will do every wrong they can think of and laugh at the truth. This will be their line of argument: "So Jesus promised to come back, did he? Then where is he? He'll never come! Why, as far back as anyone can remember, everything has remained exactly as it was since the first day of creation." (2 Pet. 3:3–4, TLB)

Peter goes on to remind us that these skeptics "deliberately" forget that God once judged the world through water and that a day was coming when he would judge it again by fire, after the return of Christ.

Isn't this the spirit we see all around us today? People today "do every wrong they can think of and laugh at the truth." And the materialistic worldview that dominates Western culture explicitly rejects the supernatural, including God. As Peter says,

> But don't forget this, dear friends, that a day or a thousand years from now is like tomorrow to the Lord. He isn't really being slow about his promised return, even though it sometimes seems that way. But he is waiting, for the good reason that he is not willing that any should perish, and he is giving more time for sinners to repent. (2 Pet. 3:8–9, TLB)

Our generation has been lulled to sleep by God's patience and misled by the long spans of time over which he works and has concluded that it's all a myth—that there is no God and no judgment to come. But Peter concludes, "The day of the Lord is surely coming . . ." (2 Pet. 3:10, TLB).

Amen. It certainly is. And it's coming soon.

2

Can We Know?

One reason few people pay much attention to the signs and prophecies that signal the return of Christ—and why few pastors preach about it—is the commonly held view that Jesus said we can't know when he is coming back. Because of that, any inquiry into the timing of Jesus' return is ruled out of bounds—we're told we just shouldn't ask such questions. And sadly, for this reason, many are missing out on the Bible's incredibly encouraging message that Jesus is coming soon.

But is it right to say that we can't know? Obviously, I don't think so, or I would not have written this book. In this chapter I'll explain why it is OK to explore the timing of Jesus' return and why I think we can know, with some precision, when it will be.

Should We Ask?

Does the Bible warn us against exploring the timing of the return of Christ? Or is it permissible to dig into God's Word to see whether we can know more about when he will come back?

Interestingly, Jesus' disciples asked this very question more than once, and on at least one occasion Jesus gave them a direct answer. Early in Matthew 24, Jesus warned his disciples that their beloved temple would soon be destroyed. In response they asked him, "When will this happen, and what will be the sign of your coming and of the end of the age?" (Matt. 24:3). In other words, they asked, "When will the temple be destroyed? And when are you coming back to usher in the new age?"

In response, Jesus delivered what we now call the Olivet Discourse, describing various events that must take place before his return: the rise of false prophets, persecution, apostasy in the church, and so on. And then in verse 14 he said, "And this gospel of the kingdom will be preached in the whole world as a testimony to all nations, and then the end will come" (Matt. 24:14). When will the end come? Jesus said only after the gospel has been preached to the whole world—to every nation.

When the disciples asked Jesus, "When are you coming back?," he answered their question.

We'll consider the Olivet Discourse throughout this book. For now, though, we want to notice that Jesus did not scold the disciples for asking, "When are you coming back?" Instead, he answered their question, providing a set of milestones for his return. He didn't name a year, but he pointed to a specific task that would have to be completed before he came back: making disciples of every nation. Certainly, the apostles didn't understand the enormity of the task—taking the gospel to every one of the thousands of people groups on earth—or how long it would take. Nevertheless, he gave them a clear picture of what they had to do before he would return.

I am doubly encouraged by this conversation. First, it reassures me to know that it is OK to ask when Jesus will return. The disciples did, and Jesus did not chastise them for doing so. And second, I'm heartened to know that if we ask, we'll receive an answer. When the disciples asked Jesus, he told them what had to happen before he came back.

"About That Day or Hour No One Knows . . ."

Later in the same conversation, Jesus tells the disciples, "But about that day or hour no one knows, not even the angels in heaven, nor the Son, but only the Father" (Matt. 24:36). This is the verse most often cited by those who would discourage us from exploring the timing of Jesus' return. Look, they say, Jesus said that even he didn't know when it would happen, so why are you wasting your time?

We'll look at this passage in more detail in chapter 10, where we'll see that "no one knows the day or hour" may be a Jewish idiom that points to the Feast of Trumpets. But for now, it's fair to say that while Jesus *was* saying that it is not possible to know *exactly* when he would return—the day or the hour—he *wasn't* saying that we can't know the *season* of his return or perhaps even the year.

Why do I say that? Because it would not make sense for Jesus to provide a long list of conditions to be fulfilled before he returns and then say, "But you can't know when that will be." What are the events he described if not road signs pointing to the time of his return? Why bother to list these events if they don't answer the question, "When are you coming back?" Jesus himself makes that point a little later in chapter 24 when he says, "Now learn this lesson from the fig tree: As soon as its twigs get tender and its leaves come out, you know that summer is near. Even so, *when you see all these things*, you know that it is near, right at the door" (Matt. 24:32–33).

In other words, Jesus said the signs he listed allow us to know when his return is "right at the door." When they have occurred, his return will be imminent.

They Asked More Than Once

Matthew 24 isn't the only time the disciples asked a question about Jesus' return. After the resurrection and just before the ascension, the disciples gathered around Jesus and asked him, "Lord, are you at this time going to restore the kingdom to Israel?" (Acts 1:6)—roughly the same question as in Matthew 24. This time, though, he gave a different answer, telling them, "It is not for you to know the times or dates the Father has set by his own authority" (Acts 1:7). What might Jesus have meant when he said, "It is not for you to know"?

For one thing, he might be saying, "You don't need to know that." The task he gives them in the next verse—to take the gospel "to the ends of the earth"—will consume their entire lifetimes and centuries more. In other words, the question "When?" isn't really relevant to them. By saying, "It's not for you to know," he's in effect saying, "It doesn't matter to you—it will be long after you've gone home."

But even more, as we've just seen, he's already answered this question, telling them that he would come back only when "every nation" has heard. Could that be why he repeats that command in verse 8? Could he be saying, "Come on, guys, I already told you this. It's a long way off. You have a lot of work to do. So quit obsessing about my return and get busy preaching."

For us today, though, the end is much closer. So perhaps for us the question "When?" takes on more relevance. If Jesus is returning very soon, we should feel greater urgency to prepare ourselves to meet our king and to share the truth with those we love who don't know him. There may not be much time left.

Like a Thief

The Bible frequently compares the return of Christ to the coming of a thief in the night. For example, Matthew 24:42–44 says,

> "Therefore keep watch, because you do not know on what day your Lord will come. But understand this: If the owner of the house had known at what time of night the thief was coming, he would have kept watch and would not have let his house be broken into. So you also must be ready, because the Son of Man will come at an hour when you do not expect him."

Jesus used this metaphor again in Revelation 3 and Revelation 16, Paul used it in 1 Thessalonians 5, and Peter used it in 2 Peter 3.

As Jesus explained, the image of a thief in the night symbolizes unpredictability. Thieves come when they are not expected. Likewise, Jesus says, "You also must be ready, because the Son of Man will come at an hour when you do not expect him."

For unbelievers, the return of the Lord will be sudden and surprising.

So that settles it, right? Jesus will come at a time we don't expect, like a thief in the night. We can't know when he's coming.

Well, maybe not. Paul uses the thief metaphor in 1 Thessalonians 5:4–6, when he says:

But you, brothers and sisters, are not in darkness so that this day should surprise you like a thief. You are all children of the light and children of the day. We do not belong to the night or to the darkness. So then, let us not be like others, who are asleep, but let us be awake and sober.

This suggests that for believers, Jesus' return is *not* unpredictable. For those in darkness—unbelievers—the return of the Lord will be sudden and surprising, like being awakened in the night by a thief breaking into your house. As Paul says in verse 3, destruction will come on them suddenly, unexpectedly, like the moment an expectant mother feels that first labor pain.

Jesus himself made this point in Matthew 24:

As it was in the days of Noah, so it will be at the coming of the Son of Man. For in the days before the flood, people were eating and drinking, marrying and giving in marriage, up to the day Noah entered the ark; and they knew nothing about what would happen until the flood came and took them all away. That is how it will be at the coming of the Son of Man. (Matt. 24:37–39)

When Jesus speaks here of "people," he means the unbelievers of that day—everyone but Noah and his family. Noah knew what was coming, but no one else believed despite Noah's preaching. They continued with life as usual—"eating and drinking, marrying and giving in marriage"—right up to the moment when judgment came. And while it's true that even Noah did not know exactly when the rain would begin to fall, he certainly knew when the ark was finished.

Revelation 3 reinforces this idea. In speaking to the church at Sardis, Jesus says, "I know your deeds; you have a reputation of being alive, but you are dead. Wake up!" The church at Sardis had fallen asleep and lost its spiritual awareness. Jesus tells them to wake up and warns that if they do not, "I will come like a thief, and you will not know at what time I will come to you" (Rev. 3:1–3). The implication is that if they do what Jesus says—wake up!—they will be "awake and sober" and will be aware of the approaching return of the Messiah.

So for unbelievers, the coming of the Lord will be unpredictable, unexpected, and shocking. But for believers—"children of the light and children of the day"—the coming of this day should not be unexpected. Just as Jesus warned in Matthew 24, Paul says, "Let us not be like others, who are asleep, but let us be awake and sober." In other words, we need to be prepared for the Lord's return, whenever it will be.

The conclusion is that for believers, the "thief in the night" metaphor is a warning to live as if Jesus' return is imminent. Jesus confirms this in Matthew 24 by immediately launching into a series of parables that illustrate the importance of vigilance and preparedness for the return of the Lord at any time. (We'll look at these parables in detail in chapter 11.)

The Thessalonians

The church at Thessalonica had been thrown into a panic. They had received a letter, purportedly from their friend Paul, telling them that the rapture had already occurred. Since they were all still present in the world, they feared they had missed it. What's more, the severe persecution they were facing had many convinced that they were already living in the final judgment—the "great and terrible day of the Lord." Hadn't God promised that they would not live through that time? What had gone wrong?

Paul had already written one letter to the Thessalonian church, in which he reiterated what he had taught them previously about the rapture. But when he heard about their concerns, he sent them a second letter in which he told them, "Don't let anyone deceive you in any way, for that day will not come until the rebellion occurs and the man of lawlessness is revealed, the man doomed to destruction" (2 Thess. 2:3).

Paul gave his friends two unmistakable milestones for the coming of "that day." He didn't say, "Don't worry about when that day will come," or "You can't know when it will come," or "It isn't any of your business when it will come," but instead directly answered their question. Had the day of the Lord already come? No, because "that day will not come until the rebellion occurs and the man of lawlessness is revealed." Since neither of those things had occurred, they didn't need to be concerned.

This is further evidence that, while we may not be able to know exactly when Jesus will come back, God has given us numerous clues—like the coming of the rebellion and the identification of the man of lawlessness—that will clearly identify the season of his return.

The End from the Beginning

Isaiah 46:9–10 is one of my favorite praise passages:

> Remember the former things, those of long ago;
> I am God, and there is no other;
> I am God, and there is none like me.
> *I make known the end from the beginning,*
> *from ancient times, what is still to come.*
> I say, "My purpose will stand,
> and I will do all that I please."

I love the way these verses affirm God's preeminence and power: "I am God, and there is none like me." And I love the way they highlight one of God's amazing attributes: that he knows "what is still to come."

But notice that, according to what God says here, he doesn't just *know* what is still to come; he also *makes it known*. In other words, God glorifies himself not only by accomplishing his purposes and doing all that he pleases, but even more by revealing beforehand what he is going to do. God calls his shots: he makes his plan, reveals his plan, and then accomplishes his plan. For example:

- He told Abraham that his descendants would be in Egypt for four hundred years (Gen. 15:13).
- He told Moses the Israelites would be in the wilderness for forty years (Num. 14:34).
- He told Jeremiah the Babylonian exile would last seventy years (Jer. 29:10).

And, amazingly, he told Daniel exactly when the Messiah would come. The prophecy of the 70 weeks in Daniel 9:25 predicts precisely the first coming of the Messiah. It is an astounding prophecy—probably the greatest example of God making "known the end from the beginning, from ancient times, what is still to come."

Our God makes known the end from the beginning, from ancient times what is still to come.

So here's the question: If God frequently reveals the timing of important events in his plan, and if he revealed the precise date of Jesus' first arrival to Daniel, is it possible that he may also have revealed the timing of his return?

Notice exactly what God says he will do in Isaiah 46: "Make known *the end* from the beginning." Make known what? *The end*—the return of Christ and the end of the age. And what does he say he will do concerning the end? *Make it known.* I think he has, and that's the point of this book—that God has revealed to us that we are living in the day of Jesus' return.

The Signs of the Times

In Matthew 16, Jesus rebuked those in his day who did not understand the signs of their times. He said, "You know how to interpret the appearance of the sky, *but you cannot interpret the signs of the times*" (Matt. 16:3).

The religious leaders came to Jesus demanding a sign, and he criticized them for not understanding the signs they had already been given—the many prophecies in the Old Testament that he had fulfilled.

In the following chapters we'll explore a number of biblical clues that indicate we are living in the day of Jesus' return. These, I think, are the signs of *our* times—the signs that reveal we're living in amazing days and that Jesus is coming soon.

PART
TWO

Unwrapping
the
Clues

And Then the
End Will Come

Suppose you had invited a friend to come to your house for dinner. If you wanted to know when she was going to arrive, who would you ask? Well, obviously, you'd ask her—she would be the one who would know the answer to the question, "When are you coming?"

And that's exactly what the disciples did, as we read in Matthew 24: they asked Jesus when he was coming back.

The disciples had been admiring the temple and its courts, when Jesus surprised them by saying, "Do you see all these things? . . . Truly I tell you, not one stone here will be left on another; every one will be thrown down." Shocked, they asked, "Tell us, . . . when will this happen, and what will be the sign of your coming and of the end of the age?" (Matt. 24:2, 3)

In response, Jesus delivers what we today call the Olivet Discourse, listing a number of events and circumstances that would occur before "his coming" and "the end of the age." But then in verse 14 he says, "And this gospel of the kingdom will be preached in the whole world as a testimony to all nations, and then the end will come." In other words, when the disciples asked Jesus, "When are you coming back?," he answered, "Only after the gospel has been preached to all nations."

To understand Jesus' answer and how it points to his imminent return, let's consider the concept of "the nations" in Scripture and how close we are to seeing his command to preach the gospel to all of them fulfilled.

God's Heart for the Nations

From beginning to end—from Genesis to Revelation—God's Word proclaims his heart for the nations. In Genesis 22:17, just after Abraham has presented Isaac for sacrifice, God promises to bless him and to multiply and prosper his descendants. And then he promises, "through your offspring all nations on earth will be blessed, because you have obeyed me" (v. 18).

When God says "your offspring" here, he is speaking of the coming Messiah, who humanly would be a distant descendant of Abraham. And when he says that "all nations" will be blessed through him, he's promising that his gift of salvation would apply to every one of them.

If we turn to the end of the Bible, in Revelation 7:9 John has a vision of "a great multitude that no one could count, *from every nation, tribe, people and language*, standing before the throne and before the Lamb." Again, we see the promise that people "from every nation" will be present at the throne of God.

That same promise is repeated over and over in Scripture. For example, in Psalm 72:17 we read, "*All nations* will be blessed through him, and they will call him blessed." Psalm 86:9 promises, "*All the nations* you have made will come and worship before you, Lord . . ." Psalm 117:1 says, "Praise the LORD, *all you nations*; extol him, all you peoples."

This same theme recurs in the Prophets. In Isaiah 49:6 (ESV), God promises that the coming Messiah will be "*a light for the nations*, that my salvation may reach to the end of the earth." In Isaiah 66:18, God says

> *From beginning to end, God's Word proclaims his heart for the nations.*

that he will "gather the people of *all nations and languages*, and they will come and see my glory." Daniel sees "one like a son of man, coming with the clouds of heaven . . . *all nations and peoples of every language worshiped him*" (7:13–14). The prophet Malachi declared, "*My name will be great among the nations*, from where the sun rises to where it sets" (1:11).

We also see the idea in the New Testament. When Peter was explaining to the leaders of the early church his decision to baptize the gentile Cornelius and his household, he said, "I now realize how true it is that God does not show favoritism *but accepts from every nation* the one who fears him and does what is right" (Acts 10:34–35).

Did you notice the words *all* and *every* repeated in these verses? Over and over again, God declares that his gospel promises apply to all nations. Every nation—all of them—will be included in his kingdom. At the Great Wedding Feast of the Lamb, when Jesus and his church are united forever, the multitude will contain men and women from every nation on earth—not one will be left out.

What Is a Nation?

When we think of the word *nation*, we think of a country, like France or India or China. But the word has a different meaning in the Bible.

In the Old Testament, the word translated "nations" is the Hebrew word *goy*. In the New Testament—and in the Septuagint, the Greek Old Testament—it's the Greek word *ethnos*, from which we get our English words ethnic, ethnicity, and so on. An *ethnos* is a group of people who share a common ethnicity, ancestry, heritage, culture, and/or language—an ethnolinguistic people group.

According to Finishing the Task (www.finishingthetask.org) there are about twelve thousand of these biblical nations scattered around the world. Some modern countries have only a few people groups, but some have many. Nigeria has over 450 "nations" within its borders. India has a similar number. Indonesia has more than three hundred.

The Origin of the Nations

So where did all these nations come from? According to Genesis 11, God created them at Babel. The Lord saw the tower the people were building to "make a name for themselves" (v. 4). Knowing they were acting in disobedience to his command to "fill the earth,"

the Lord "confuse[d] their language so they [would] not understand each other" and "scattered them over the face of the whole
earth" (vv. 4–8).

Genesis 11:1 tells us that before this time, "the whole world
had one language and a common speech." There were no *ethnos*—
all the peoples of the earth were unified with a common language.
But after this, they were divided and scattered.

God's Plan for the Nations

Even though it was God who divided the nations, his plan has
always been to unify them again under Jesus Christ through the
gospel. In Ephesians 2:13–16 we read:

> But now in Christ Jesus you who once were far away have
> been brought near by the blood of Christ. For he himself
> is our peace, *who has made the two one and has destroyed
> the barrier, the dividing wall of hostility*, by setting aside in
> his flesh the law with its commands and regulations. *His
> purpose was to create in himself one new man out of the two,
> thus making peace*, and in one body to reconcile both of
> them to God through the cross, by which he put to death
> their hostility.

Paul here was speaking specifically about Greeks and Jews, but
the passage applies to every people group on earth. Just as God
united the Jews and Greeks in Corinth into one new body, he is
creating "one new man"—the church—that includes people from
every one of the world's twelve thousand nations. And in that one
body he is reconciling all of them "to God through the cross, by

which he put to death their hostility." In Ephesians 3, Paul describes this truth as "the mystery made known to me by revelation . . . that through the gospel the Gentiles are heirs together with Israel, members together of one body, and sharers together in the promise in Christ Jesus" (vv. 3, 6).

God's plan has always been to reunify the world's nation under Jesus Christ through the gospel.

Think about how amazing that claim is—that through Jesus Christ God plans to unify twelve thousand people groups and "put to death" the hostility that divides them from one another. Sadly, people everywhere hate and fear others. Many think we have a corner on racism here in the United States, but enmity between people groups is common around the world. God will bring tremendous glory to himself one day by putting an end to all of that hatred and racism through Christ.

Consider how much glory it will bring God to win such a lopsided victory. When he is finished, not one nation will be left as the exclusive possession of the enemy—the final score will be 12,000 to 0. At one time Satan had dominion over every nation on earth, but in the end, God will have won back disciples from every one of them.

By the way, the world is constantly striving to accomplish this same goal—the unification of the world's peoples—apart from God. That's the impulse behind world empires—to create a secular worldwide kingdom. It's the motivating force behind the modern utopian globalist instinct. Ultimately this desire will be briefly fulfilled, under the antichrist, during the tribulation. But then God's authentic kingdom will come and sweep that false kingdom away.

The Great Commission

In Matthew 28:19, Jesus commands his apostles to "go and make disciples of all nations." Today we call this command the Great Commission.

As we've seen, this command has deep biblical roots. When Jesus spoke these words, he ordered his church to fulfill all the promises God had made concerning the nations—especially the promise that his salvation would not just be for the Jews but for "all nations."

Rick Warren, pastor of Saddleback Church and leader of Finishing the Task, talks about the "3 Bs" of the Great Commission: Believers in every people group, the Bible in every language, and a Body of Christ—a church—in every village and neighborhood. He says that we'll know for certain that we've completed the Great Commission task when we've accomplished all three of these goals.

The church has been working for two thousand years to fulfill the Great Commission, and much has been accomplished. But exactly where do we stand in the effort to make disciples of "all nations?"

Believers in Every People Group

Out of twelve thousand people groups in the world, today we know with confidence that there are believers in over 11,500 of them.

About six thousand of the twelve thousand would be classified as "reached," meaning that they have a meaningful Christian population. Nearly that many would be considered "unreached," meaning that while they have some Christian presence, it is small—less than 2 percent of the population. But a few hundred groups remain that are called "unengaged," meaning that no one has ever been to them with the gospel—there has never been a single Christian among them. (Opinions differ about these numbers and even how to measure them. My data is based on the work of Finishing the Task and my own firsthand knowledge gained as the managing partner of the Finishing Fund.)

Today, there are only a few hundred people groups left who have never heard the gospel.

As you might expect, these remaining unengaged groups are mostly very small—typically just a few thousand people. They are located in remote, difficult, dangerous places: in vast deserts, high mountains, and deep jungles. Many are Muslim groups. Some are aggressively hostile to outsiders. Most are not literate. They are the last groups for a reason!

But over the last few years the number of unengaged groups has fallen dramatically. In 2005, there were more than 3,500 unengaged people groups with a total population of over 700 million people. Even as recently as 2015, there were still more than 1,400 groups with no known Christians. But today, there are only a few hundred unengaged groups remaining, and hundreds of people groups are being engaged with the gospel each year. By God's grace, I believe the church will reach all of the remaining groups by the end of 2022, or shortly thereafter. We're very close to the finish line.

Stories of the Unengaged

For the last several years I have been privileged to lead the Finishing Fund, a partnership of generous Christians who are giving together to send the gospel to the world's last few unengaged people groups. So far, we've helped send missionaries to more than 450 people groups, and we've already seen the first new believers in more than 320 of those groups.

You'll find the story of the first known believer in the history of the world from one of those groups, the Gregh, on the next page. You'll find similar stories about other first believers throughout this book. I have changed the names and places in these accounts to protect the missionaries and new believers, but the stories are 100 percent true—these things really happened in just the last couple of years. They tell the story of how God is working in our day to bring the Great Commission to completion.

How Is This Happening?

A significant factor in the rapid spread of the gospel is good research; today we have a much better idea who these people are and where they are located. Another is improvement in the techniques of church planting and disciple making, especially among oral peoples. Another key, of course, is the advance in technology in the past century: automobiles and motorbikes, airplanes, radio, television, the Internet, and so on. All of these help people and

THE GOSPEL COMES TO

The Gregh

The Gregh are a minority people group living in five villages in the remote mountains of a small central Asian country. In two thousand years, no one had ever gone to the Gregh with the gospel of Jesus Christ. To the best of anyone's knowledge, there had never been even one Gregh believer.

But in March 2018, after much prayer and fasting, a team of believers from that country made the treacherous journey over the mountains to one of the five Gregh villages. The team had asked God to lead them to a person of peace among the Gregh.

As they approached the village, they encountered a man name Abdul walking beside the road with his cattle. They stopped, engaged him in conversation, and began sharing the gospel. As Abdul heard the good news for the first time, he began to weep, confessing that he had been deeply troubled by his sin and had not known how to be free of his burden of guilt. On the spot, Abdul accepted God's gift of forgiveness. He became the first known Gregh believer—ever!

Abdul immediately invited the team to his house, where they shared the gospel with his family. They now know Jesus, and Abdul's home has become the site of the first Gregh church. By God's grace the good news is spreading, bringing hope to a people who before only knew slavery to religious ritual, with no forgiveness, no peace, no assurance, and no freedom.

The gospel has come to the Gregh.

information move more freely and quickly to the places who have never heard.

Another element is the emergence of the indigenous church as a missionary force. All around the world, the local church is stepping up to the challenge of engaging these last people groups with the gospel. They are sending national missionaries who are culturally similar to the unengaged and who share a language with them. These "near-culture" missionaries are able to take the gospel more effectively and at a much lower cost than Western missionaries.

> *The Holy Spirit is working around the world to gather in a great end times harvest.*

But the most important reason for the rapid expansion of God's kingdom into the unengaged groups is the powerful movement of the Holy Spirit. He is working around the world, in places where until recently the name of Jesus had never been heard, to gather in a great end times harvest. We've all heard stories of missionaries in the old days who would give their whole lives to a place and only see a handful of converts, if any. Today, missionaries often see the first new believer in an unengaged place within the first week or so after their arrival—sometimes on the first day. That's because the Holy Spirit has already been in that place, preparing the hearts of those he has chosen to receive the good news.

And Then the End Will Come

This brings us back to Matthew 24:14 and Jesus' promise that "this gospel of the kingdom will be preached in the whole world as a testimony to all nations, and then the end will come." When will the end come? Jesus said after the gospel has been preached to "all nations." If we're only a few years away from crossing this finish line, could it also be true that we're only a few years away from the return of Christ? I believe it is.

Bible and Body

The goals for the second and third Bs—the Bible in every language and a Body in every place—are a little further away but are nevertheless very close. Every Tribe Every Nation, a network of Bible translation organizations, is working to assure that "by 2033, every tongue, tribe and nation will have access to God's Word and its life-changing hope." The Global Alliance for Church Multiplication (GACX), a collaboration of church planting ministries, is striving toward the goal of five million new churches—one church for every thousand people throughout the unchurched world—by 2025.

So even if Jesus waits until the Bible has been translated into every language and churches have been planted in every place, by God's grace we don't have long to wait.

It Won't Be Long

I believe the church is only a handful of years away from fulfilling Jesus' command to "go and make disciples of all nations." Only a few hundred people groups remain that have not heard, and hundreds of groups are hearing for the first time every year. Translators are working hard to make the Scripture available in every language. Hundreds of thousands of new churches are being planted in every corner of the world. The Holy Spirit is working powerfully around the world to gather in those whom God has chosen, even in places where the light of the gospel has never been seen before.

In fairness, we can't be sure exactly where the Great Commission finish line lies. Peter tells us that "the Lord . . . is patient . . . not wanting anyone to perish, but everyone to come to repentance" (2 Pet. 3:9). Even after the gospel has been preached to every people group, Jesus may tarry so that every possible person has the chance to hear.

But once we've crossed that finish line—once there are disciples in every one of the earth's people groups—the door will be open for the first time in two thousand years to the return of Christ. Jesus said that the gospel would be preached to all nations, "and then the end will come." We can't know for certain if that will be immediately, but based on Jesus' promise, the clock will be ticking for his return, and he could come at any time. I think it will be soon.

THE GOSPEL COMES TO

The Ceesa

The Ceesa people live in an isolated oasis—more than sixteen hours by road from their country's capital city. They have a unique desert culture and their own distinct language.

There is evidence that the Ceesa may once have been Christians, but since the 1300s they have been Sunni Muslims. As far as anyone knows, there has not be a single Ceesa Jesus follower in seven hundred years.

Mohammed is a Ceesa Berber farmer who makes his living growing dates and olives. One day he saw a man picking and eating olives from a tree near his house. Rather than chase the stranger away, he introduced himself and welcomed him into his home for some delicious dates.

The man, named Ali, was a Christian who had come to Ceesa to share the good news. As he was eating, he began telling his host about Isa. When Mohammed heard the name, his eyes got big. He told Ali, "I have seen Isa in my dreams! I want to know more about him!" Ali continued to explain the good news to Mohammed, and soon Mohammed gave his life to Jesus. He became the first Ceesa believer in hundreds of years!

Today there are more than fifty believers among the Ceesa Berbers, worshiping God in five house churches. Seven leaders have been identified and are being trained to lead the work God has started there.

The gospel has come to the Ceesa.

Behold the Fig Tree

The modern state of Israel is a miracle—an unequivocal fulfill-ment of ancient prophecies that in the end times God would regather his chosen people into their ancestral land. The reestablishment of Israel is also an unmistakable sign that we are living in the last days, and may provide an important clue about the timing of the return of Jesus Christ.

The simple fact that the Jewish people have endured as a people through nearly two thousand years of being scattered among the nations is amazing. There is a story that when King Louis XIV of France asked Blaise Pascal, the great French philosopher, to give him proof that miracles occur, Pascal answered, "Why, the Jews, your Majesty—the Jews."[3] The French philosopher Jean-Jacques Rousseau compared the Jewish nation with the lost civilizations of Rome, Sparta, and Athens, and said, "Though destroyed, Zion has not lost her children. They mingle with all nations but are never lost among them; they no longer have leaders, yet they are still a nation; they no longer have a country and yet they are still citizens."[4]

The survival of the Jews as a people for so long, sprinkled as a tiny minority around the world, in the face of enormous persecution, is so unlikely as to be unbelievable, except as an act of God.

But for that group to be regathered into a new nation, in their original homeland, despite enormous worldwide political opposition, is truly preposterous—so unlikely that it can only be explained as a miracle. Theologian Robert Newman observed,

> What are the probabilities that a people group will be globally dispersed, yet retain its identity for centuries independently of a homeland, survive almost continual persecution and harassment, and then return to reestablish their nation? That a globally dispersed group would return to their native land and resettle it after two thousand years is *unique in history.*[5]

"Unique in history" means that it literally has never happened before. And for that reason, until about a century ago, many people dismissed the possibility that Israel would be reestablished. It just seemed impossible. Even today—shockingly—some still resist the idea that the modern nation of Israel has any prophetic importance, despite the many ways it fulfills prophecy.

The Prophecy

But of course those who believe the Bible know that God had always promised to reestablish Israel. In fact, the regathering of Israel is the most frequently prophesied event in the Old Testament.

The diaspora—the dispersal of the Jewish people into the nations around the world—was clearly prophesied in the Old Testament. In Deuteronomy 28, when God lays out the blessings that will flow to the Israelites if they obey his commands and the curses that will fall on them if they do not, we read, "If you are not careful to do all the words of this law that are written in this book . . . *the LORD will scatter you among all peoples, from one end of the earth to the other . . .*" It goes on to say "And among these nations you shall find no respite, and there shall be no resting place for the sole of your foot . . ." (vv. 58, 64, ESV). This prophecy describes precisely the state of the Jews for centuries before the founding of modern Israel in 1948.

The regathering of Israel is the most frequently prophesied event in the Old Testament.

But while God clearly promised that he would scatter the people if they would not obey him, a few chapters later, in Deuteronomy 30, he promises that eventually he will regather Israel into its homeland. He says,

The LORD your God will restore your fortunes and have compassion on you and *gather you again from all the nations where he scattered you.* Even if you have been banished to the most distant land under the heavens, *from there the LORD your God will gather you and bring you back. He will bring you to the land that belonged to your ancestors, and you will take possession of it.* He will make you more prosperous and numerous than your ancestors. (vv. 3–5)

God has begun to fulfill the promise of this more-than-three-thousand-year-old prophecy over the last two centuries. Through a series of improbable historical events—including two world wars and the Holocaust—and despite nearly uniform worldwide opposition, the Jews now possess the land God gave to their ancestors.

Jews have emigrated to modern Israel from more than seventy countries.[6] They have literally been gathered "again from all the nations," even "the most distant land under the heavens." More than three million Jewish people have left their homes and emigrated to Israel since 1948[7]—so many that, in many countries, there are now few if any Jews remaining. Today, about 6.8 million Jews, or more than 46% percent of the world's Jewish population, live in Israel[8]—up from only about sixty thousand in 1918[9]. And, as promised, Israel has become one of the world's most prosperous countries, ranking around twentieth in per-capita GDP.[10]

The restoration of the Israelites to their ancestral land has always been, in a sense, inevitable, because of the promise God gave Abraham in Genesis 17:8: "The whole land of Canaan, where you now reside as a foreigner, I will give as an *everlasting possession* to you and your descendants after you . . ." Even though God removed his people from the land for many centuries, it was always certain that they would one day return to claim it again. After all, God had promised it to them as an "everlasting possession."

Spiritual Revival

God's work among the Jewish people has not ended with the formation of the modern nation of Israel. Deuteronomy 30:6 promises that after Israel is regathered as a nation, the Jews will experience spiritual rebirth: "The Lord your God will circumcise your hearts and the hearts of your descendants, so that you may love him with all your heart and with all your soul, and live."

Several other Old Testament passages make clear that this heart change for the Jews will follow their return to their homeland. For example, Ezekiel 36:24–28 promises:

> For I will take you out of the nations; *I will gather you from all the countries and bring you back into your own land.* I will sprinkle clean water on you, and you will be clean; I will cleanse you from all your impurities and from all your idols. *I will give you a new heart and put a new spirit in you; I will remove from you your heart of stone and give you a heart of flesh.* And I will put my Spirit in you and move you to follow my decrees and be careful to keep my laws. Then you will live in the land I gave your ancestors; you will be my people, and I will be your God.

These passages predict that Israel will first be regathered as a nation and then will be granted spiritual rebirth. This idea is illustrated by the dramatic vision recorded in Ezekiel 37, where the prophet witnesses the resurrection of a great army in the valley of the dry bones. As God begins to work, the bones are first assembled into bodies, step by step, but at first are not alive: "there was no breath in them." These lifeless bodies represent present-day secular Israel—a body reassembled piece by piece over time but lacking spiritual life. But then, God commands Ezekiel to prophesy, "Come, breath, from the four winds and breathe into these slain, that they may live," and—amazingly—"breath entered them; they came to life and stood up on their feet—a vast army" (Ezek. 37:9–10).

God explains Ezekiel's vision in 37:12–14. He says that he will "open your graves and bring you up from them; *I will bring you back to the land of Israel*" and then, after they have been regathered, he "*will put [his] Spirit in you and you will live . . .*"

> Israel will first be regathered as a nation and then will be granted spiritual rebirth.

God's promise of revival for his people is still to be kept. Most students of the end times believe that God will fulfill that promise at the return of the Messiah. Zechariah 12:10 says that on the day the Lord returns, he will "pour out on the house of David and the inhabitants of Jerusalem a spirit of grace and supplication" and that they will "look on me, the one they have pierced, and they will mourn for him as one mourns for an only child, and grieve bitterly for him as one grieves for a firstborn son."

An Even Greater Miracle

Prior to the resurrection, God's greatest miracle was the exodus and, in particular, the parting of the Red Sea. At the critical moment, God divided the sea so that his people could cross over on dry land, escaping the Egyptians and gaining their freedom from slavery. God's Word declares over and over that it was by this miracle that his relationship with his people would be known. For example,

Deuteronomy 5:6 declares, "I am the LORD your God, who brought you out of Egypt, out of the land of slavery."

But in Jeremiah 23:7–8, God predicts that in the future, he will be known for an even greater feat:

> "So then, the days are coming," declares the LORD, "when people will no longer say, 'As surely as the LORD lives, who brought the Israelites up out of Egypt,' but they will say, 'As surely as the LORD lives, *who brought the descendants of Israel up out of the land of the north and out of all the countries where he had banished them.*' Then they will live in their own land."

One day, God says, the regathering of the children of Israel will outshine even the miracle of the exodus. The regathering will be seen as an even greater miracle than the parting of the Red Sea.

In Defense of His Name

God declares that he will do this in defense of his own name. Ezekiel 36:22 (NLT) says, "I am bringing you back, but not because you deserve it. *I am doing it to protect my holy name, on which you brought shame while you were scattered among the nations.*"

God had promised that his people would possess the land he had given them forever. But over the centuries, while the people were under judgment and scattered among the nations, God's enemies accused him of being unable to keep that promise. So, God says to "protect [his] holy name"—to "show how holy [his] great name is"—he is going to "gather you up from all the nations and bring you home again to your land."

Jerusalem

Zechariah 8:7–8 promises that when the Jews are regathered "from the countries of the east and the west" that they will "live in Jerusalem." We've witnessed the fulfillment of this specific prophecy in recent years.

The original Plan of Partition for British Palestine anticipated that Jerusalem would be an international city, controlled neither by Israel nor its Arab neighbors. But in the 1948 War of Independence, Israel captured West Jerusalem, which soon became the nation's official capital (although it was not internationally recognized as such). Jordan captured East Jerusalem, including the old walled city and the Temple Mount. Later, in the 1967 Six-Day War, Israel captured East Jerusalem as well, restoring the city to Jewish control, and in 1980, Israel passed the Jerusalem Law, declaring Jerusalem the "complete and united" capital of Israel, which it remains to this day. Once again, we see God's prophecies being fulfilled fully and precisely.

Opposition

Ezekiel 36:1–7 predicts that the re-creation of Israel would be strongly opposed by the surrounding nations, specifically mentioning Edom as a proxy for all the surrounding Arab nations. History certainly has validated that prophecy.

Even before Israel was formed, Arab opposition led to a significant part of the British mandate—land that was originally intended to be part of the new nation of Israel—being set aside for a Palestinian state, the nation of Jordan. As soon as Israel was established in 1948, the surrounding nations fought a war in an attempt to exterminate the new country—a war in which they were defeated. They tried again in 1967 (the Six-Day War) and again in 1973 (the Yom Kippur War), each time suffering defeat and losing territory to Israel. And the effort by the Arabs (and other Muslim nations, such as Iran) to destroy the state of Israel has continued through the 1982 and 2006 Lebanon wars, the first and second Intifadas, and the Gaza War of 2008.

That Israel has prevailed and even prospered in the face of these continual attacks fulfills yet another biblical prophecy. According to the prophet Amos, once they have been regathered, the Jewish people will never be driven out of their land again. Amos 9:15 promises, "I will plant Israel in their own land, never again to be uprooted from the land I have given them."

That Israel has prospered in the face of continual attacks fulfills yet another biblical prophecy.

Today, opposition to Israel is growing worldwide—the whole world seems to be turning against it. Even as some Arab states are normalizing relations with Israel, others, especially Iran, are doubling down in their antagonism.

The Bible predicts that opposition will increase and that sometime between now and the return of Christ coalitions of nations will launch attacks against God's people. Ezekiel 39 predicts one such invasion and promises God will miraculously defend his people. And Zechariah 12:3 promises, "On that day, when all the nations of the earth are gathered against her, I will make Jerusalem an immovable rock for all the nations."

Wasteland Brought to Life

Deuteronomy 29:23–24 prophesies that the land of Israel would become a desolate and barren wasteland after God drove his people from it: "The whole land will be a burning waste of salt and sulfur—nothing planted, nothing sprouting, no vegetation growing on it. It will be like the destruction of Sodom and Gomorrah . . . which the LORD overthrew in fierce anger." The destruction will be so catastrophic that "all the nations will ask: 'Why has the LORD done this to this land? Why this fierce, burning anger?' "

And in fact that is a remarkably accurate description of the land as it was in 1948, when Israel was reborn. Mark Twain, who traveled to the Holy Land in 1867, described it like this in his book *The Innocents Abroad*:

- "It is a blistering, naked, treeless land."
- "Of all the lands there are for dismal scenery, I think Palestine must be the prince."
- "It is a hopeless, dreary, heart-broken land."
- "Palestine sits in sackcloth and ashes . . ."

But the Bible also promised that once God's people returned to the land, God would turn it from a wasteland into a garden. Ezekiel 36:34–35 says that one of the signs that the regathering would be an act of God is that "the desolate land will be cultivated instead of lying desolate" and promises the people who witness it will say, "This land that was laid waste has become like the garden of Eden." Likewise, Isaiah 27:6 promises, "In days to come Jacob will take root, Israel will bud and blossom and fill all the world with fruit."

Today those prophecies are being fulfilled. If you've traveled to Israel, you know that while parts of the country are arid, much of it is now a rich, fertile agricultural garden. Israel has today become a major source of agricultural innovation and is now a major exporter of food including fresh citrus[11] and other fruits. Truly, "This land that was laid waste has become like the garden of Eden."

Many Other Prophecies

There are many other Old Testament prophecies of the return of the Jews to their homeland. But the examples I've cited should be enough to prove that God long ago prophesied what we see occurring in our lifetimes. In these last days, God's people are being regathered from around the world into the land he promised them would be their possession forever.

The Prophecy of the Fig Tree

Jesus told his disciples that the regathering of Israel would be an important sign about the imminence of his return. In Matthew 24:32–34 he says,

> Now learn this lesson from the fig tree: As soon as its twigs get tender and its leaves come out, you know that summer is near. Even so, when you see all these things, you know that it is near, right at the door. Truly I tell you, this generation will certainly not pass away until all these things have happened.

Wait, you might be thinking, *what does a fig tree have to do with the regathering of Israel?* Well, the fig tree is an important symbol of Israel throughout the Bible. In Hosea 9:10 God says of Israel, "When I found Israel, it was like finding grapes in the desert; when I saw your ancestors, it was like *seeing the early fruit on the fig tree.*"

Likewise, in Jeremiah 24:2–10 we read that the prophet was given a vision of two baskets of figs: "One basket had *very good figs*, like those that ripen early; the other basket had very bad figs, so bad they could not be eaten." God tells Jeremiah that these figs were symbolic of two groups in Judah, one of which he would "watch over . . . for their good" and "bring . . . back to this land" and the other that he would destroy by "sword, famine and plague."

Jesus also used the fig as a symbol for God's people in one of the parables recorded in Luke 13. And later, at the very end of his ministry, Jesus cursed a fig tree that he found fruitless—likely symbolizing that he had lost hope that the fig tree of Judah would bear fruit.

So when Jesus says, in Matthew 24:32, "learn this lesson from the fig tree," he's speaking metaphorically of Israel. He's saying that when you see Israel, the fig tree, beginning to green up, you'll "know that it [his return and the end of the age] is near, right at the door." In other words, when Israel begins to regather, Jesus' return will be near.

> The Bible says that when Israel begins to regather, we can know that Jesus' return is near.

Then he adds this: "Truly I tell you, this generation will certainly not pass away until all these things have happened" (v. 34). "This generation" may refer to those who heard Jesus speak, but it may instead mean those who are privileged to witness the greening of the fig tree—the regathering of the nation of Israel. With that in mind, we can see that "all these things" would refer to the events surrounding Jesus' return.

In other words, Jesus promised that the generation that witnessed the restoration of Israel would not pass away before he returned.

Summer Is Near

We can't be sure exactly what Jesus meant by a generation. Did he mean that at least one person who was alive to witness the establishment of Israel would still be alive when he returned? Or was he describing some interval of time—some span of time called a "generation"? Either way, it has now been over 70 years since Israel was established—and more than 50 years since Israel took possession of Jerusalem—and we are certainly approaching the end of the generation that witnessed those amazing events. The fact that Israel is being regathered, in keeping with God's many promises to do so, has started the clock, and while we can't know for certain when the alarm will ring, we can know that it is going to be very soon.

THE GOSPEL COMES TO The Topang

As T and B wound up the dirt road toward the Topang village, they prayed for favor. They had come as covert missionaries to survey the Topang people, one of the many tiny people groups hidden in the isolated mountains of a small Asian country. Like many of those groups, the Topang are animists who live in fear of the spirit world. Like most of them, they had never heard the Good News. No one had ever gone to the Topang with the gospel.

When the men arrived, they met a woman named Yon, a village leader. As the men inquired about life in the village, Yon told them of their many problems, illnesses, and addictions. She said, "We feed the spirits, but we're still poor, sick, and sad. I don't think the spirits can really save us." Sensing an opening, T and B began to tell Yon about the One who really can save. They explained how Jesus came into the world, how he lived and died, and how one day he will come again. After hearing the gospel, Yon decided to become a follower of Jesus, and T and B led her in a prayer to receive Christ. She became the first known Topang believer—ever!

Immediately, Yon called her husband and children to hear the story. As T and B shared the gospel with them, they also placed their faith in Christ! By God's grace, this family's faith will grow into a movement of disciples among the Topang, and they will be set free from their lives of hopelessness and fear.

The gospel has come to the Topang.

The Abomination

The prophet Daniel was one of the greatest men who has ever lived—a man described in the Bible as being "highly esteemed" by God. Because of Daniel's faithfulness and righteousness, God was pleased to reveal amazing prophecies through him. Daniel's book is filled with astounding visions that reveal many future events, some of which have already occurred and some which are still to be fulfilled.

In this chapter we'll consider the prophecies of the first and second comings in Daniel 9 and 12. We'll start by testing whether God revealed the year of Jesus' first coming to Daniel. And then we'll consider whether Daniel 12 likewise predicts the year of Jesus' return.

The Prophecy of the First Coming

One of the main themes of the book of Daniel is the promise of a coming Messiah. In Daniel 2, he's revealed as the "rock . . . cut out, but not by human hands" that "struck the statue on its feet of iron and clay and smashed them" (v. 34). In Daniel 7 he's "one like a son of man" who "was given authority, glory and sovereign power; all nations and peoples of every language worshiped him" (vv. 13, 14).

And then in Daniel 9:25–26, we read:

> "Know and understand this: From the time the word goes out to restore and rebuild Jerusalem until the Anointed One, the ruler, comes, there will be seven 'sevens,' and sixty-two 'sevens.' It will be rebuilt with streets and a trench, but in times of trouble. After the sixty-two 'sevens,' the Anointed One will be put to death and will have nothing."

The speaker here is the angel Gabriel, who has been sent by God to Daniel in response to Daniel's amazing pastoral prayer of repentance in Daniel 9:4–19.

Gabriel lays out a timeline for Daniel of coming events. The timeline begins with a specific event—"from the time the word goes out to restore and rebuild Jerusalem"—and ends with another specific event: "until the Anointed One, the ruler, comes . . ."

The Anointed One

We can be sure that "the Anointed One" mentioned in verses 25 and 26 is the Messiah. The Hebrew word here, *mashiach*, is the word for "messiah," and several translations render "Anointed One" as Messiah. So that much is clear—Gabriel is providing a timeline for the first coming of the Messiah.

The Interval

Gabriel tells Daniel that "there will be seven 'sevens,' and sixty-two 'sevens'" between the issuing of the edict "to restore and rebuild Jerusalem" and the coming of the Messiah. Most evangelical scholars believe that Gabriel's "sevens" describe seven-year periods of time—weeks of years, so to speak. So "seven 'sevens,' and sixty-two 'sevens'" describes seven plus sixty-two, or sixty-nine, seven-year periods. Multiplying by 7 yields 483 years—the interval between the beginning and end of the timeline.

Gabriel revealed to Daniel the exact timing of the first coming of the Messiah.

The prophecy further states that "after" the end of the sixty-nine sevens, the Anointed One will be "will be put to death and will have nothing." This is widely regarded to be a prophecy of the crucifixion.

The Start of the Timeline

Gabriel says that the interval begins "from the time the word goes out to restore and rebuild Jerusalem." He's referring to a command that had not yet been issued that would allow the Jews to return to their country and rebuild their city.

In verse 25b he says, "It will be rebuilt with streets and a trench, but in times of trouble." Commentators think that "streets" describes the interior parts of the city and that "a trench" should be interpreted broadly to describe external defensive fortifications such as a moat or a wall.

So we're looking for a command, issued by a Babylonian or Persian king, that permitted the Jews to return to Jerusalem and rebuild the city and its fortifications. We know from history that such a command was actually issued—the Jews did return to Judah and rebuild Jerusalem and its wall. If we can figure out when this command was issued, we'll know the starting point of Daniel's prophecy.

The Decree

The challenge is that there were actually four such commands, recorded in Ezra 1, Ezra 6, Ezra 7, and Nehemiah 2. But only the fourth order, given by the Persian King Artaxerxes to Nehemiah and recorded in Nehemiah 2, satisfies Gabriel's prophecy perfectly. In verse 5, Nehemiah asks Artaxerxes to "send me to the city in Judah where my ancestors are buried so that *I can rebuild it*." And in verse 8 Nehemiah says, "Because the gracious hand of my God was on me, the king granted my requests."

Further, recall that Gabriel said that the city would be rebuilt in "times of trouble," which could very well refer to the opposition Nehemiah and his men faced from Sanballat in their rebuilding project. And we know from the book of Nehemiah that his work was exclusively focused on the reconstruction of Jerusalem's wall—exactly the work specified in Gabriel's prophecy.

A Question of Dates

Nehemiah 2 tells us this command was issued in the twentieth year of the reign of Artaxerxes, which most scholars say was 445 BC. But the Greek historian Thucydides suggests an alternative date.

According to Thucydides, the exiled Athenian general Themistocles fled Greece in 474 BC and met Artaxerxes in Persia shortly thereafter, in 473 BC, *just after* Artaxerxes ascended to the throne. If that's correct, it would imply that Artaxerxes became king around 475 BC and that Nehemiah's decree was issued twenty years later, in 455 BC, not in 445 BC.[12]

Doing the Math

Four hundred eighty-three years after 455 BC is 29 AD, which is certainly a possible date for the "coming" of the Messiah. If Jesus' "coming" was marked by his arrival in Jerusalem for Holy Week, 29 AD would be year of his crucifixion, which is early but within the accepted range. If his coming was marked by an earlier event—such as his baptism or his sermon in the synagogue in Capernaum—his arrival in 29 AD would set his crucifixion later, in 32 or 33 AD—again, within the accepted range.

Artaxerxes's decree in Nehemiah 2 is a perfect match for the command Gabriel describes in Daniel 9. If that command was issued in 455 BC instead of 445 BC, it seems that Gabriel revealed to Daniel the exact timing of the first coming of the Messiah. Amazing.

Prophesying the Second Coming

So it seems that Gabriel revealed to Daniel the exact year of Jesus' first coming. But how about the second coming? Did God also disclose that to Daniel?

Daniel 12 focuses on the events of the end times. Daniel was visited by an angelic figure, who told him, "At that time . . . there will be a time of distress such as has not happened from the beginning of nations until then" (v. 1)—an evident prophecy of the tribulation. The angel said, "Multitudes who sleep in the dust of the earth will awake: some to everlasting life, others to shame and everlasting contempt" (v. 2), predicting the coming resurrection of the dead. In verse 4 (NASB), the angel told Daniel, "Many will go back and forth, and knowledge will increase," which identifies two defining characteristics of the last days: increasing human movement and increasing knowledge. We'll consider those prophecies in chapter 7.

Did God also reveal the timing of the second coming to Daniel?

In verse 8 (NLT) Daniel says, "I heard what he said, but I did not understand what he meant. So I asked, 'How will all this finally end, my lord?'" Daniel was confused, so he asked for more information. In response, the angel says,

"Go your way, Daniel, because the words are rolled up and sealed until the time of the end. Many will be purified, made spotless and refined, but the wicked will continue to be wicked. None of the wicked will understand, but those who are wise will understand.

"From the time that the daily sacrifice is abolished and the abomination that causes desolation is set up, there will be 1,290 days. Blessed is the one who waits for and reaches the end of the 1,335 days." (vv. 10–12)

I have taught the book of Daniel three times, and each time, when I've reached the end, I've had to confess that verses 11 and 12 were a mystery. Many try to connect this passage with the 1,260-day period described in Revelation 11 and 13 and the "time, times, and half a time" presented elsewhere in Daniel, and I suppose that's possible. But neither that explanation nor any other I've read has satisfied me—they're just too contrived.

As I began to study the subject of this book, though, I came across a better explanation of these verses—one that makes more sense than any I've heard before and that seems to point with great precision to the timing of the second coming of the Messiah. Here is a summary of that interpretation:

- The time that the daily sacrifice is abolished refers to the Babylonian conquest of Jerusalem.
- The "1,290 days" is a period of 1,290 years beginning with the end of the sacrifice.
- The "abomination that causes desolation" describes the Dome of the Rock, which was built on the Temple Mount 1,290 years after the Babylonian conquest.
- The "1,335 days" is a period of 1,335 years that began with the construction of the Dome and that ends around 2030 AD.

In other words, this prophecy echoes the Daniel 9 prophecy of the first coming and points to the return of Christ in the next few years.

Let's dive in and see if that explanation holds together.

One Event or Two?

The first question about this prophecy is this: Do "the time that the daily sacrifice is abolished" and "the abomination that causes desolation is set up" describe two events that occur at the same time or events separated by 1,290 days? In most English translations, these two phrases are joined with an "and," leading to the conclusion that they are contemporaneous. But other translations suggest that these events are separated in time. For example, the Common English Bible translates Daniel 12:11 like this:

> There will be one thousand two hundred ninety days *from the time* the daily sacrifice is stopped to the setting up of the desolating monstrosity.

The Contemporary English Version and the New Century Versions are similar.

In these translations, it's clear that verses 11 and 12 are similar to the passage from Daniel 9: they present an interval of time with a defined beginning and ending. The beginning is "the time that the daily sacrifice is abolished," the end is "the abomination that causes desolation is set up," and the interval is "1,290 days." But in these verses, there is also a second interval, "1,335 days," after which those who have endured will be blessed.

The Starting Point

Let's begin with the initial event: "From the time that the daily sacrifice is abolished." As with the Daniel 9 passage, there are numerous guesses about what event this may be describing. But put yourself in Daniel's shoes. When he heard the phrase "the time that the daily sacrifice is abolished," what would have come to his mind? He immediately would have thought of the Babylonian conquest of Jerusalem, which he had lived through as a young man. He knew the temple had been destroyed and that the sacrifice had been abolished. So given the context and the audience, I think it's likely that when the "man dressed in linen" said "from the time that the daily sacrifice is abolished," he meant when the Babylonians ended it.

The Babylonians conquered Jerusalem in three waves over a period of about eighteen years. The conquest began in 605 BC, when Daniel was taken into exile, and ended in 587 BC, when the Babylonians finally destroyed the city. In between, in 597 BC, the Babylonians besieged Jerusalem, exiled large parts of the population (including King Jehoiachin), and installed Zedekiah as puppet king. You can read about these events in Daniel 1 and in 2 Kings 24 and 25.

To Daniel, "from the time the daily sacrifice is abolished," meant when the Babylonians ended it.

At what point during this eighteen-year period was the daily sacrifice abolished? We really can't know for certain. What we can know with confidence is that there was a day in one of those years on which the daily sacrifices stopped. For simplicity's sake, from here on we're going to assume that sacrifice ended in 597 BC— which I think is the most likely date—but when you see that date in the following paragraphs remember that it represents a range of possible dates.

The 1,290 Days

We saw that in Daniel 9 "sevens" or "weeks" described periods of seven years. Is it possible that "days" has the same meaning in this passage, so that 1,290 *days* represents a period of 1,290 *years*?

If we begin with 597 BC and come forward in time 1,290 years, we arrive at 694 AD. (There is no year zero, so we have to add one year.) Is there anything happening in Jerusalem or on the Temple Mount at that time that might fulfill the prophecy of an "abomination that causes desolation?"

Interestingly, at that exact time the Dome of the Rock (the Qubbat al-Sakhrah), an Islamic shrine, was being build and dedicated on the Temple Mount, on the site of the temple and the Holy of Holies. Most scholars believe construction of the Dome was begun around 684 AD and was completed in 692 AD, but some think construction began in 692 AD and was completed a few years later, perhaps in 694.[13] Either way, the dates fall within the range predicted by Gabriel's prophecy.

Abomination

But does the Dome of the Rock qualify as "the abomination that causes desolation?" It's probably not what comes to mind when you think of the abomination, so let's take a minute to explore that idea.

First, it's important to understand that the "abomination that causes desolation" has had several fulfillments in history and will have at least one more:

- The first "abomination that causes desolation," prophesied in Daniel 8 and Daniel 11, was fulfilled in 167 AD when the Greek king Antiochus Epiphanes IV erected an idol of Zeus in the Holy of Holies and sacrificed a pig on the altar.
- A second one took place when the Roman general Titus besieged and destroyed Jerusalem in 70 AD. According to the Jewish historian Josephus, Titus erected a large golden

eagle—the symbol of Roman power and domination—over the temple gates. Many believe that this event fulfilled Jesus' warning in Matthew 24:15–16.

- The final instance of the abomination that causes desolation was prophesied in Daniel 9 and Daniel 11: speaking of "the ruler who is to come," Gabriel says, "He will put an end to sacrifice and offering. And at the temple he will set up an abomination that causes desolation, until the end that is decreed is poured out on him" (Dan. 9:27). The fulfillment of this prophecy will take place during the tribulation when the antichrist will erect "an image in honor of the beast who was wounded by the sword and yet lived" (Rev. 13:14) and force the entire world to worship it, on penalty of death.

So instead of asking, "Could the Dome of the Rock be *the* abomination that causes desolation?," we should instead ask, "Could the Dome of the Rock be *an* abomination that causes desolation—not the only fulfillment of the concept but one of several instances of it?"

The Dome of the Rock fulfills the requirements of being an abomination and causing desolation.

The Hebrew word translated "abomination" is *shiqquts*, which is derived from the word *shaqats*, to detest, and means disgusting, filthy, detestable, or detestable thing. *Shiqquts* is a generic term for anything that is reprehensible to Yahweh. It is used frequently in the Old Testament to refer to idols or to the idolatrous practices of pagan religions: detestable idols.

Does the Dome of the Rock qualify as *shiqquts*? Inside the Dome of the Rock, on the walls of the octagonal arcade, you'll find an inscription in Arabic, which claims, among other things, that

- God has no son,
- there is no Trinity,
- Jesus is merely a messenger or prophet, and
- Jesus has not yet been raised from the dead.[14]

Do those claims rise to the level of *shiqquts*? I would argue that they do, especially when you consider where they are found.

Desolation

The angel describes not just an abomination, but an abomination that causes desolation. The Hebrew word translated "desolation" is *shamem*. It is translated in the Bible as "desolate," "desolated," "desolation," "make desolate," and so on. In English, the word *desolation* means a state of complete emptiness or destruction, devastation, or ruin. It can also mean to make unfit for use or habitation or to defile.

Does the Dome of the Rock fulfill this part of the angel's description? Certainly, the presence of a pagan shrine on the Temple Mount, over the Holy of Holies, is defiling. And because the Dome is there, the temple cannot be rebuilt and the daily sacrifice cannot be resumed. In that way its presence renders the location "unfit for use."

In other words, the Dome of the Rock is literally an abomination that causes desolation, and it was built on the site of the temple 1,290 years after the "end of the sacrifice," just as the man in linen prophesied.

The 1,335 Days

That leaves us with the final part of the Daniel 12 prophecy, in verse 12: "Blessed is the one who waits for and reaches the end of the 1,335 days." We'll assume as we did before that days represent years: that when the man in linen speaks of 1,335 *days* he means 1,335 *years*.

The next question is this: Does the 1,335 days overlap the 1,290 days, or does it follow them? Remember that the context here is the angel answering Daniel's question, "My lord, what will the outcome of all this be?" And remember that "all this" refers to the angel's prophecies of tribulation, resurrection, and judgment—the "times of the end."

Given that context, we're going to say that the 1,335 years follow the 1,290 years. Why? Because we know that the tribulation and resurrection of the dead did not occur in the early eighth century AD, forty-five years after the construction of the Dome. We're still waiting for those things to take place today.

Doing the Math

As shown in table 1, if we begin with the year 694 AD and come forward 1,335 years, we arrive at 2029. If instead we begin with the accepted date for the Dome's dedication—692 AD—adding 1,335 years brings us to 2027. The range of possible dates begins in 2021 and ends in 2039. Could one of these be the year for the events described in Daniel 12 and for the return of Christ?

Table 1: The Daniel 12 Prophecy

End of the sacrifice?	Scripture	+1,290 Years	+1,335 Years
605 BC	2 Kings 24	686 AD	2021 AD
599 BC		692 AD	2027 AD
597 BC	2 Kings 24	694 AD	2029 AD
587 BC	2 Kings 25	704 AD	2039 AD

Remember that the context of Daniel 12 is "the time of the end," so it makes sense that the terminal date of prophecy of days in verses 11 and 12 would point to that time. And the angel's promise in verse 12—"Blessed is the one who waits for and reaches the end of the 1,335 days"—intersects with several ideas we talk about elsewhere in this book. As we saw in chapter 1, the return of Christ in the last days is described as the "Blessed Hope" of those who follow Jesus. As we learned in chapter 4, the return of Christ as the promised King on That Day will be a great blessing to the remnant of Israel who have survived the tribulation. Last, the angels' words, "the one who waits for and reaches the end," echoes Jesus' words in Matthew 24 that "the one who stands firm to the end will be saved."

One More Time

Daniel 12 contains several important prophecies of the end times. In verses 11 and 12, Daniel receives a prophecy that

- the daily sacrifice would end;
- 1,290 "days" later, an "abomination that causes desolation" would appear; and
- those who endure 1,335 "days" would be blessed.

We decoded this prophecy in the following way:

- "The end of the sacrifice" refers to the Babylonian conquest.
- The Babylonians conquered Judah between 605 and 587 BC.
- The daily sacrifice ended in that period, most likely in 597 BC.
- We assume that, as in Daniel 9, "days" represents years.
- 1,290 years after 597 BC is 694 AD—exactly the time the Dome of the Rock was constructed on the Temple Mount.
- The Dome qualifies as an abomination causing desolation and thus fulfills the second element of the prophecy.
- The 1,335 "days" follows the 1290 "days."
- 1,335 years after 694 AD is 2029 AD.

Because we can't know for certain the year when the Babylonians put an end to the daily sacrifice, we cannot know for sure which year the prophecy points to for the return of Christ. But that's just as well—it's not important that we know exactly. What matters is that this important clue from Daniel 12—like all the others we consider in this book—suggests that it's going to be very soon!

THE GOSPEL COMES TO

The Wulu

The Wulu people are farmers and fishermen who live on an island in a Muslim Asian country. For centuries they have practiced a kind of syncretic Sunni Islam, combining Muslim practices with witchcraft.

As far as anyone knows, there has never been a single Christian among the Wulu. In fact, no one has ever even tried to tell them the good news of Jesus Christ.

Rashid is a Wulu fisherman and witchdoctor—a man who practices healing using black magic. He is a generous man, well respected among his family and friends.

One day recently, Rashid met a man offering products to increase his shrimp production. Their conversation led to a discussion about life after death. The man showed Rashid from the Hadith that Isa Al-Masih will judge the world at the end time and shared from the Bible that Isa is the Savior of the world. Rashid was shocked and surprised, and his spiritual eyes were opened. Not many days later, he gave his life to Jesus. He became the first Wulu believer—ever!

Rashid immediately surrendered his amulets and charms to be burned and began sharing his new faith. Many family members, including his wife and children, have now been baptized. Several of Rashid's friends have also believed, and one woman has been delivered from demon possession. Today more than forty Wulu are followers of Jesus.

The gospel has come to the Wulu.

6

A Week of Millennia

Have you ever noticed that in the Bible, things happen in sevens? Think about the seven days of creation; the seven Hebrew feasts; the seventy "sevens" of Daniel 9; the seven statements of Christ from the cross; and the seven churches, seven angels, seven seals, and seven plagues of Revelation.

Interestingly, there is a widely and long-held idea that biblical history is governed by this same pattern of sevens—that history will play out over a "week" of six thousand-year "days" followed by a thousand-year Sabbath millennium. If that's true, we're living in the last days, at the end of that six-thousand-year period and at the dawn of the great thousand-year Sabbath.

A Pattern of Sevens

The biblical significance of seven is, of course, rooted in the seven days of creation. Genesis 2:2–3 says,

By the seventh day God had finished the work he had been doing; so on the seventh day he rested from all his work. Then God blessed the seventh day and made it holy, because on it he rested from all the work of creating that he had done.

Because God finished his creation work and rested on the seventh day, seven is widely considered to be the number of God and to represent perfection and completion.

In the Old Testament, God mandated that the number seven would resound through the calendars of his people. The seven-day week, which is founded on the biblical seven-day creation week, is literally a weekly reminder that God is the creator of and the Lord over all things.

> God mandated that the number seven would echo through the calendars of his people.

In the Ten Commandments, God commanded his people to observe a Sabbath day of rest and worship every seventh day. From its earliest days, the church has followed a similar pattern, observing the Lord's day once a week on Sunday.

The Sabbath Year

What's more, God mandated that every seventh year in the Hebrew calendar would be a Sabbath year. In Leviticus 25, God tells Moses that after the Israelites enter the Promised Land, "the land itself must observe a sabbath to the Lord." The people would be allowed to plant and harvest for six years, *"but in the seventh year* the land is to have a year of sabbath rest, a sabbath to the Lord." In that seventh, Sabbath year, agricultural activity was forbidden. The people could eat whatever the land produced on its own and they could pick with their hands, but they were not permitted to plow, sow, cultivate, or harvest—"the land [was] to have a year of rest" (Lev. 25:1, 4, 5).

By the way, the Israelites apparently never actually observed the Sabbath year. Much later, God would prophesy through Jeremiah that the Babylonian captivity would last seventy years—according to Leviticus 26, one year for each Sabbath year that the Jews had failed to observe since coming to the Promised Land.

The Jubilee

The pattern of sevens goes even further. In Leviticus 25, God instructed that every seventh Sabbath year—every forty-ninth year—would be a special Year of Jubilee. During that year, there was to be no agricultural activity, Hebrew slaves and prisoners were to be freed, debts were to be forgiven, and land that had been sold returned to its family of original ownership.

A Week of Millennia

What if this pattern goes even deeper? From ancient times many have believed that the pattern of sevens also applies to history as a whole—that God's plan is for this creation to have a span of seven "days." Instead of representing years or centuries, though, these "days" would represent millennia—thousand-year periods. Like the original creation week, this "week of millennia" would consist of six thousand-year "days" plus a seventh thousand-year "day" of rest.

So according to this theory, world history as described in the Bible would have a seven-thousand-year span.

Many leading figures of the early church, including Irenaeus, Hippolytus of Rome, Methodius of Olympus, Lactantius, and Augustine believed that world history would span six thousand years, followed by the return of Christ and the establishment of his thousand-year kingdom. The noncanonical but influential Epistle of Barnabas also endorses this idea.

The seven-thousand-year model also finds support in Jewish scholarship, including the Talmud, the Midrash, and the Zohar, among others.[15] While none of these sources is inerrant or authoritative, together they show that the theory has a long history of broad support.

What's more, twice in Scripture—in Psalm 90:4 and 2 Peter 3:8—we are told that for God a day is like a thousand years and a thousand years is like a day, which lends support to the day–millennium linkage.

From ancient times many have believed that the pattern of sevens applies to history as a whole.

In addition, Scripture explicitly supports the idea of a thousand-year period of Sabbath rest at the end of history. In Revelation 20 we read about the thousand-year reign of Christ and his saints on the earth, following his return. Satan will be bound during this time, unable to influence the world toward evil. Elsewhere in Scripture we learn that this will be a time of unprecedented peace, justice, righteousness, and prosperity—a true Sabbath rest from the world as we know it.

The Hosea Prophecy

An even more intriguing biblical hint affirming the seven-thousand-year tradition is found in the book of Hosea. In this beautiful book, Hosea describes God's coming judgment against Israel and Judah on account of their unfaithfulness to him, but also offers hopeful promises of regathering and restoration. In Hosea 5:14–15 we read,

> For I will be like a lion to Ephraim,
> like a great lion to Judah.
> *I will tear them to pieces and go away;*
> I will carry them off, with no one to rescue them.
> *Then I will return to my lair*
> *until they have borne their guilt and seek my face—*
> in their misery
> they will earnestly seek me."

The speaker in these verses is God, foreshadowing the coming judgment of Israel and Judah. He says that he will "tear them to pieces" and "carry them off, with no one to rescue them," and then depart from them: "I will . . . go away . . . and return to my lair until they have borne their guilt and seek my face."

Many think this prophecy was fulfilled at the time of the crucifixion, after the Jews had rejected their Messiah, or perhaps in 70 AD, when the Romans destroyed Jerusalem, driving the Jews from the Promised Land and scattering them around the world. They would argue that during this period of diaspora God withdrew from his people in judgment for their rejection of the Messiah, waiting for a day when they will repent and "seek his face."

Then in Hosea 6:1–2 we read:

"Come, let us return to the LORD.
He has torn us to pieces
    but he will heal us;
he has injured us
    but he will bind up our wounds.
After two days he will revive us;
    on the third day he will restore us,
    that we may live in his presence.

Now the speaker is Israel and Judah collectively, expressing their desire to repent and return to the Lord. They speak acceptingly of God's judgment—"he has torn us to pieces" and "he has injured us"—but also hopefully of his grace and mercy in response to their repentance: "he will heal us," "he will bind up our wounds," "he will revive us," "he will restore us."

> *God promised in Hosea 6 to revive his people "two days" after he has turned away from them.*

When will this happen? How long will it take for the relationship between God and his people to be restored? Hosea 6:2 says, "After two days he will revive us; on the third day he will restore us, that we may live in his presence." Two days after what? The most reasonable guess would be two days after he has fulfilled his promise from Hosea 5 to "go away" and "return to my lair."

And could it be that, as Psalm 90:4 and 2 Peter 3:8 suggest, those two days represent two thousand years? In other words, that in these verses God is promising to revive his people two thousand years after the departure of the Messiah or the destruction of the temple? And that he further promises to restore them and live in their presence for another thousand years after that?

If so, we're living in the day of the completion of this prophecy. When did Jesus "go away"? If it was when he ascended, two thousand years later would be somewhere between 2028 and 2033. And if that range applies to Christ's return to Israel—the second coming—then we would expect the rapture to be seven years earlier, or somewhere between 2021 and 2026. Even if the starting point for the two days of Hosea 6 is later—perhaps as late as 70 AD—we're still within a few decades of the end of the two-thousand-year period.

Does It Fit?

How well does this "six-thousand-year-plus-one-thousand-year" model of history fit the biblical account? The widely held consensus is that, according to a literal reading of the Bible's history and genealogies, God created Adam about 4000 BC. Archbishop Usher, who developed the best-known biblical chronology, put the year at 4004 BC, but others, including Martin Luther, Johannes Kepler, and Sir Isaac Newton, independently arrived at very similar dates.[16] The different dates produced by different scholars suggest that it may not be possible for us to know the exact biblical date for Adam's creation, but because they all arrive at approximately the same date, we can have confidence that the Bible places it within a narrow span of one hundred years or so, about six thousand years ago.

The Hebrew Calendar

Interestingly, though, the official Hebrew calendar is slightly at odds with these calculations. According to the Hebrew calendar, I am writing this chapter in the year 5780 AM, or anno mundi, Latin for "in the year of the world"—in other words, since the creation. And while 5780 is pretty close to 6000, the difference is big enough to raise questions. Have the Christian biblical scholars missed something?

The origin, history, and mathematics of the Hebrew calendar are very complex—well beyond the scope of this book. However, there is a strong argument that the Hebrew calendar contains at least one major error of about 165 years due to a miscalculation of the interval between the destruction of the First and Second Temples.[17] If this argument is correct, the current actual date anno mundi would be 5945—much closer to the estimates of the Christian scholars. Correcting additional smaller possible errors might bring the Hebrew calendar even closer to the Christian reckoning.

Three Eras

The roughly six thousand years of biblical history are often divided into three eras: two thousand years from Adam to Abraham, two thousand years from Abraham to the first coming of Christ, and two thousand years from Christ's first coming to his return. It's that last bit that should interest us the most, because it corresponds so closely to the prophecies of Hosea 5 and 6 and suggests that we're living in the days of the Lord's return.

Figure 1: A Week of Millennia

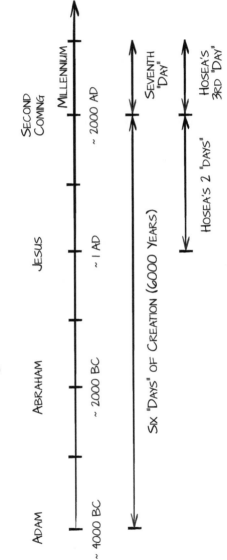

Seventy Jubilees

Let's consider one last idea before we wrap up this chapter. We've seen how the pattern of sevens and seventies recurs in the calendar of God's people: seven days to a week, seven weeks to a Sabbath year, and seven Sabbath years to a Jubilee. Some think there is also a pattern of seventy Sabbath years that define a series of 490-year periods in the history of God's people: 490 years from Abraham to the Exodus, 490 years from the Exodus to Solomon's Temple, 490 years from Solomon's Temple to the Babylonian Exile, and 490 years from the return from the Exile to the crucifixion.

One interesting thing we haven't considered is whether there might be significance to the seventieth Jubilee.

Scholars largely agree that the counting of Sabbath years (and thus Jubilee years) began when the Israelites entered the Promised Land, as God ordered in Leviticus 25. Many evangelical scholars believe that the Jews entered Canaan in 1406 BC. Therefore, the first Sabbath year would have been seven years later, or 1399 BC, and the first Jubilee would have been in 1357 BC.

So when will the seventieth Jubilee take place? Seventy times forty-nine years is 3,430 years, and adding 3,430 years to 1406 BC yields 2025. (Again, there is no year zero, so you have to add one when you cross over from BC to AD.)

We don't want to put too much weight on this clue. For one thing, nowhere in the Bible is any significance assigned to the seventieth Jubilee; it may be important, but it also may mean nothing. Even with that caveat, though, to me the idea that the seventieth Jubilee might be right around the corner is thought-provoking, especially when seen in the light of everything else we've discussed in this chapter. And it may be one more hint that something amazing is about to happen.

Summing Up

A recurring pattern of sevens is imbedded in God's holy calendar. It echoes the seven days of creation and serves as a reminder that he is the creator of and sovereign Lord over all things. There is a widely and long-held tradition in the church and among Jewish scholars that the history of the world will follow this pattern and comprise a "week" of seven millennia: six thousand years of human history followed by a thousand-year millennial reign of Christ.

According to the biblical chronology, we are now at or very near the end of that first six-thousand-year period. What's more, we're very near the end of the "two days" since the departure of the Messiah prophesied in Hosea 5 and 6, and we may be about to experience the seventieth Jubilee year. While it's not possible to pin the dates down to one particular year, each of these clues supports the theme of this book: that Jesus is coming back very soon.

THE GOSPEL COMES TO

The Yardima

The Yardima are a tiny people group who live high in the highest mountains. The center of Yardima culture is their temple, where even today the infant daughters of the poor can be purchased and sacrificed to appease the demons they worship. As far as anyone knows, there has never been a single Jesus follower among the Yardima. In fact, no one has ever even tried to tell them the good news of Jesus Christ.

But recently, Ruth, a young mother and Jesus follower, heard about the Yardima and felt God calling her take the gospel to them. So she and her husband traveled by bus for two and a half days to the Yardima village. Once there, they walked and prayed around the temple for three days, asking God to connect them to a person of peace.

Finally, a teenager named Ona ventured out. Ona's parents were temple musicians, and she lived with them on the temple grounds. The women began talking, and Ruth could sense Ona's deep depression. She told Ona that Jesus would heal her spirit if she would believe in him. Ona cried out to Jesus, and instantly her depression vanished. She became the first known Yardima believer—ever!

Later, Ruth and Ona prayed for Ona's paralyzed brother, and God healed him as well. As a result, Ona's parents also came to Christ, and today more than fifty Yardima believers meet weekly in a house church—incredibly, on the grounds of the temple!

The gospel has come to the Yardima.

7

The Days of Noah

S o far, we've looked at a number of prophecies that point to the
soon return of Christ: the imminent completion of the Great
Commission, the regathering of Israel and the Parable of the Fig
Tree, the prophecy of Daniel 12:11–12; and the three-day prophecy of Hosea 5 and 6.

In this chapter, we'll consider three more clues that indicate
that we're living in the days of Jesus' return:

1. Jesus' prediction that the last days would be like the days of
   Noah and the days of Lot
2. The prophecy in 1 Thessalonians 5 that the day of the Lord
   will come when people are crying out for peace and safety
3. The prophecy from Daniel 12:4 of increased human travel
   and knowledge in the last days

The signs we're examining in this chapter are different from the
others we've considered, but they are just as important. They don't

point to a specific year, but we can be sure that Jesus will not come back until they have been fulfilled. And as we'll see, they all have been—some quite dramatically.

As in the Days of Noah

In Luke 17:26–30, Jesus compares the time of his return with the days of Noah and the days of Lot:

> *"Just as it was in the days of Noah, so also will it be in the days of the Son of Man.* People were eating, drinking, marrying and being given in marriage up to the day Noah entered the ark. Then the flood came and destroyed them all.

> *"It was the same in the days of Lot.* People were eating and drinking, buying and selling, planting and building. But the day Lot left Sodom, fire and sulfur rained down from heaven and destroyed them all.

> *"It will be just like this on the day the Son of Man is revealed.*

In chapter 2, we saw how these prophecies predict that for the lost, Jesus' coming will be sudden and unexpected—like the coming of a "thief in the night." Just as in the days of Noah and Lot, people will be living their normal lives—"eating and drinking, buying and selling"—right up until the time judgment begins.

But these verses also suggest something important about the moral condition of the world at the time of the end. The two examples Jesus cites—the world before the flood and the cities of Sodom and Gomorrah, where Lot lived—were both characterized by extreme depravity, wickedness, and godlessness.

In Genesis 18:20, the Lord tells Abraham that the sins of Sodom and Gomorrah are "very grave." Ezekiel 16:49–50 describes Sodom in this way: "She and her daughters were arrogant, overfed and unconcerned; they did not help the poor and needy. They were haughty and did detestable things before me."

Likewise, in describing the world just before the flood, Genesis 6:5 says, "The Lord saw how great the wickedness of the human race had become on the earth, and that every inclination of the thoughts of the human heart was only evil all the time."

We may not be there quite yet, but is there any doubt that our generation—especially in the West—is similarly identified by our great evil? In the United States, over 62 million babies have been aborted since the *Roe v. Wade* decision in 1973—a level of infant sacrifice to the god of sexual freedom that the demon Molech could only dream of.

When Jesus says that the days of his return will be like the days of Noah, he's describing a time of extreme wickedness.

Since the 1960s, the sexual revolution has led to enormous increases in adultery and premarital sex. According to one survey, "Premarital sex is normal behavior for the vast majority of Americans,"[18] and the rate of sex before marriage is rapidly increasing in non-Western countries as well.[19]

While pornography is as old as mankind, today we're living through an epidemic of porn, amplified by technology. Every kind of unspeakable pornography is available at a whim, thanks to the Internet. And tragically, pornography has become one of the West's major exports.

We've seen the rise of homosexuality and have become the first culture in the history of the world to sanction same-sex marriage, which is a direct challenge to God's establishment of marriage as the union of one man and one woman. Our cultural elites have embraced transsexualism and are attempting to abandon binary sexuality, in defiance of God's fundamental pronouncement that he "created mankind in his own image, in the image of God he created them; *male and female he created them*" (Ge. 1:27).

And all of these things have happened in just the last few years—it's as though a tidal wave of sexual immorality had swept over our culture.

But it's not just sexual morality that has collapsed. In 2 Timothy 3:1–5, the Apostle Paul warns

> But mark this: There will be terrible times in the last days. People will be lovers of themselves, lovers of money, boastful, proud, abusive, disobedient to their parents, ungrateful, unholy, without love, unforgiving, slanderous, without self-control, brutal, not lovers of the good, treacherous, rash, conceited, lovers of pleasure rather than lovers of God—having a form of godliness but denying its power. Have nothing to do with such people.

That's a long list, and some of the things Paul mentions are more evident today than others. But don't "lovers of money," "boastful," "disobedient to their parents," "unforgiving"—think of cancel culture—and "lovers of pleasure" all vividly describe our modern Western culture?

In Romans 1, Paul describes the world that surrounded the early church in the pre-Christian Roman Empire. Sadly, that passage also describes the post-Christian culture of our time. He says:

> For although they knew God, they neither glorified him as God nor gave thanks to him, but their thinking became futile and their foolish hearts were darkened. *Although they claimed to be wise, they became fools* . . .

> Therefore God gave them over in the sinful desires of their hearts to sexual impurity for the degrading of their bodies with one another. They exchanged the truth about God for a lie, and worshiped and served created things rather than the Creator—who is forever praised. Amen. (vv. 21–25)

The passage goes on to say that God "gave them over to shameful lusts" and "to a depraved mind so that they do what ought not to be done." He says,

> They have become filled with every kind of wickedness, evil, greed and depravity. They are full of envy, murder, strife, deceit and malice. They are gossips, slanderers, God-haters, insolent, arrogant and boastful; they invent ways of doing evil; they disobey their parents; they have no understanding, no fidelity, no love, no mercy. Although they know God's righteous decree that those who do such things deserve death, they not only continue to do these very things but also approve of those who practice them (vv. 29–32).

That's a sad and frightening picture of the postmodern culture that surrounds the church today. Every word Paul uses to describe the pre-Christian culture he lived in applies more and more to our world as well. For instance, could there be a more apt description of the elites who guide our culture than "Although they claimed to be wise, they became fools"?

As bad as things are, they can get worse (and seem to be!). We still haven't reached the place where "every inclination of the thoughts of the human heart was only evil all the time" (Gen. 6:5). But there's little doubt that our culture increasingly fits Jesus' description of the last days as being like the days of Noah and Lot.

Peace and Safety

In 1 Thessalonians 5:1–3, Paul says

> Now, brothers and sisters, about times and dates we do not need to write to you, for you know very well that the day of the Lord will come like a thief in the night. *While people are saying, "Peace and safety,"* destruction will come on them suddenly, as labor pains on a pregnant woman, and they will not escape.

This verse warns that the "day of the Lord"—the return of Christ in judgment—will come on the world suddenly, like a "thief in the night." At the very time people are crying out for "peace and safety," Paul says, the judgment will come.

Although the final fulfillment of this prophecy lies in the future, the cry for "peace and safety" is already characteristic of our culture today.

Safetyism

In their book *The Coddling of the American Mind*, Jonathan Haidt and Greg Lukianoff describe what they call safetyism: "a culture or belief system in which safety has become a sacred value"—in other words, a cult of safety. In the safetyism cult, they say, "'Safety' trumps everything else, no matter how unlikely or trivial the potential danger."[20] Barry Glassner, author of *The Culture of Fear: Why Americans Are Afraid of the Wrong Things*, says, "Most Americans live in what is arguably the safest time and place in human history, and yet fear levels are high . . ."[21]

> *Even though we live in arguably the safest time and place in history, our culture is obsessed with safety.*

We see safetyism everywhere these days. Think about helicopter parents who will not allow their children out of their sight for fear of an accident or abduction. When I was a first grader, I walked alone four or five blocks to school, as did most of my classmates. Our parents thought nothing of it. Today you'd probably be arrested for letting your kid do that. When I was a little older, I'd jump on my bike and go to the park or to a friend's house for the day. My parents wanted to know where I was, but I was otherwise free to come and go. Most kids today have nothing like that kind of freedom. Lukianoff and Haidt call today's approach "paranoid parenting" and say, "Members of iGen (born in 1995 and later) are having very different childhoods than kids in previous generations had, and are also suffering from much higher levels of anxiety and depression."[22]

Or consider the warning labels—"this product contains a chemical known to cause cancer" and "do not stand above this step"—that appear on seemingly every product these days. Those labels, many of which are ridiculous, are symbolic of our culture's obsession with identifying and eliminating every possible risk from life.

Think about the proliferation of safety features in automobiles. I remember the first car my parents owned that had safety belts, sometime in the 1960s. (We thought they were so cool—like an airplane!) Today, cars not only have seatbelts but also airbags, and my wife's latest car has a slew of smart features such as adaptive cruise control, automatic emergency braking, blind spot monitors, lane change warnings—the list goes on and on. (I call the car "The Nanny" because of its annoying supervision of my driving.) Do these features make the car safer? Absolutely. But their presence is evidence of our culture's escalating emphasis on safety.

If you don't believe me, start listening for the words *safety* and *safe* in media. They're everywhere. I recently heard an ad for a car dealer on the radio telling me how "safe" I'd be buying from them. I'm not sure I'd ever even thought about safety in the context of shopping for a car, but there they were selling it to me. During a recent football game I watched an ad from a major home improvement chain promoting its commitment to safety. It said, "Safety. It's not a fad or a trend. It's not even a priority. Priorities shift and change. At [*name of chain*] we believe safety is more than that. To us, it's a value. . . . Safety unites us." There's nothing wrong with a home improvement store telling you that they value safety, but this ad didn't mention low prices or great selection or the assistance its expert staff could provide with your project—it promoted only safety. Fascinating.

If you want to understand how safetyism permeates our culture, test your reaction to the various examples I've mentioned. Did you find yourself pushing back, thinking that something I named was actually a reasonable precaution? Perhaps you're right, but can you see from these examples how the pursuit of perfect safety is intensifying?

The most stunning and frightening instance of safetyism has been the worldwide response to COVID-19. The fear of this disease has led countries around the world to shut down their economies and impose drastic restrictions on the liberties of their citizens. While COVID-19 is real, it does not compare to the truly terrifying diseases of old like plague and smallpox—or even to the Spanish Flu of 1918, which killed between 1 and 5.5 percent of the world's population.[23] To put that in perspective, if COVID-19 were as lethal as the Spanish Flu, it would have killed between 78 million and 429 million people worldwide.[24] The current estimate is that perhaps two million people have died from COVID-19, meaning that it is from forty times to *over two hundred times* less dangerous than the Spanish Flu.[25] And yet we've been overcome by an exaggerated, unreasonable fear that the coronavirus is going to kill us all and by a frantic pursuit of safety at all costs. Sadly, COVID-19 safetyism has even infected our churches.

The cult of safetyism plays on the most primal human emotion: the fear of death. As Christians, we are—or should be—set free from this fear, as Hebrews 2:14–15 declares: "Since the children have flesh and blood, he too shared in their humanity so that by his death he might break the power of him who holds the power of death—that is, the devil—and *free those who all their lives were held in slavery by their fear of death.*"

But as Western culture has moved away from Christianity, this freedom from the fear of death has been lost, and more and more we see it expressed in the incessant pursuit of perfect safety.

Peace

Peace can mean the absence of war, and over the course of the last few decades we've witnessed a burgeoning worldwide peace movement that may be a fulfillment of the 1 Thessalonians 5 prophecy. Ultimately, it will likely be this desire for peace that permits the antichrist to seize worldwide power.

But when Paul says the last days will be characterized by the pursuit of peace, I think he has something different in mind: not peace between warring nations but inner peace, tranquility, and personal comfort.

The Greek word translated "peace" in this verse is *eirene*, and it means peace, quietness, rest, or peace of mind. In English, the word *peace* can mean "a state of tranquility or quiet, specifically, freedom from disquieting or oppressive thoughts or emotions."

We see our post-Christian culture's fear of death expressed in the increasing pursuit of perfect safety.

Our culture is overwhelmed by disquieting and oppressive thoughts and emotions—things like fear, shame, regret, anger, anxiety, and depression. Since we are unmoored from God, we're on our own against these enemies. So we turn to meditation, medication—both legal and illegal—positive thinking, yoga, physical fitness, Kondo-ing, aroma therapy, Zen Buddhism, CBD oil, healing crystals, and who knows what else to provide the inner peace we crave.

Of course, all of those things are counterfeits. They cannot meet our need for inner peace because they lack power over the circumstances that disquiet us, and so they cannot replace the one true source of peace: a relationship with Jesus Christ, who is the Lord over every circumstance. On the night before he was crucified, Jesus told his disciples, "Peace I leave with you; my peace I give you. I do not give to you as the world gives. Do not let your hearts be troubled and do not be afraid" (John 14:27).

The Bible teaches that the insatiable pursuit of inner peace through anything other than the gospel will continue and increase as the day of Jesus draws near.

Israel and Palestine

We also hear the cry "peace and safety" from the world's political leaders as they pursue a solution to the Israeli–Palestinian conflict. If only the parties could agree to a two-state solution, these leaders contend, then Israel and the whole world would enjoy peace and safety. For example, when President Obama addressed the United Nations General Assembly in 2012, he called for "two states living side-by-side in *peace and security*."[26] President Trump's proposal for a solution to the Israeli–Palestinian conflict "recognizes it is time for a new approach to achieve *peace, security*, dignity, and opportunity for Israel and the Palestinian people."[27]

Ultimately, the pursuit of "peace and safety" in the Middle East will result in a treaty between Israel and the antichrist, described in Daniel 9:27, guaranteeing Israel's peace and safety. That treaty, which will be signed at the beginning of the seven-year great tribulation, will surely be a fulfillment of Paul's prophecy from 1 Thessalonians 5.

The Tossing of the Sea

In Luke 21 Jesus delivers the Olivet Discourse, explaining to the disciples the events that would precede his return. In verses 25 and 26 he says, "On the earth, nations will be in anguish and perplexity at the roaring and tossing of the sea. People will faint from terror, apprehensive of what is coming on the world." He's describing a time of intense global turmoil. Probably, Jesus is speaking of things that are still in the future: perhaps a worldwide calamity, following the rapture, that sets the stage for the rise of the antichrist; perhaps the actual events of the tribulation; or perhaps the world's reaction to the tribulation judgments themselves.

But the worldwide reaction to COVID-19 gives us at least a sense of the state of mind Jesus had in mind. Certainly, "nations will be in anguish and perplexity" is an apt description of the panic that has characterized the response to COVID by governments around the world. And is it difficult to imagine how the COVID scare—or some similar event—could lead to the rise of a powerful world leader like the antichrist? It seems like all he would have to do is promise people safety from their fears.

The False Prophets of Old

In the days before Israel and Judah were carried off into bondage, God sent prophets to accuse the people of their sin, urge them to repent, and warn them about what was to happen if they did not. But these voices of God were opposed by false prophets who told the people not to worry—that God was still with them and judgment was not coming.

In Jeremiah 6:14, God mocks these false prophets, saying, "They dress the wound of my people as though it were not serious. 'Peace, peace,' they say, when there is no peace."

I expect as the day of the Lord draws near we will see modern-day versions of these false prophets of old. Like their ancestors, they will reassure the people that they have nothing to fear—right up until the time Jesus returns.

The Signs of Technology

In chapter 5, we explored the possibility that Daniel 12:11–12 prophesies the timing of the return of Christ. But there is another fascinating prophecy in Daniel 12 that also points to our day as the season for his return. Daniel 12:4 (NASB) says, "Many will go back and forth, and knowledge will increase." This verse describes two essential characteristics of the last days: increasing travel and migration and increasing knowledge. Both are vividly descriptive of our day and age.

"Many Will Go Back and Forth"

"Many will go back and forth" predicts a dramatic increase in travel in the last days—a prophecy that is amazingly characteristic of our times.

Consider that until the invention of the railroad around 1800, the fastest any human being had ever traveled was the speed of a galloping horse or a fast sailboat—maybe 30 miles per hour. This made long-distance travel slow and painful, and as a result for most of human history few people traveled more than a short distance from their birthplace. During the nineteenth century, though, railroad speeds increased to as much as 80 miles per hour, and people began to travel greater distances.

But it was the invention of the airplane that really got people moving. By the 1930s, DC-3 airliners were routinely flying passengers at the shocking speed of 200 miles per hour. With the invention of the jet engine in the 1940s, the speed of travel quickly increased to more than 600 miles per hour—twenty times faster than anyone had ever traveled just 150 years earlier.

(For a few years in the '70s, '80s, and '90s, air travel was even faster. The Aérospatiale/BAC Concorde cruised at Mach 2.0, or about 1,350 miles per hour. It could make the trip from Paris to New York in just under four hours, departing Paris at 10:30 a.m. local time and arriving in New York at 8:25 a.m.—literally outflying the sun across the surface of the earth. In 1993, wanting to experience supersonic flight, I booked my return from a European business trip on Concorde. The flight was expensive, luxurious, and amazingly brief, but surprisingly there was no real sense of speed. In fact, the only noticeable difference from any other flight was that the curvature of the earth was clearly visible through the window, a consequence of the very high altitude at which Concorde flew. That was worth seeing!)

Jet airplanes have opened the door to a dramatic increase in world travel. In 1950 there were a total of 25 million international tourist arrivals worldwide. By 2018 that number had increased 56-fold, to 1.4 billion.[28]

Trips that would have taken weeks or even months just a few hundred years ago can now be completed in just a day or two. Consider one example. When William Cary, the father of modern missions, traveled to India from England in 1793, the journey took five months. But on my most recent trip to India, I boarded a flight in Newark at 9:00 p.m. and arrived at about the same time the next evening in Delhi, a fourteen-hour journey—astoundingly fast and beyond the wildest imagination of people just a few decades earlier.

While few have experienced it, it's worth mentioning that we also live in the era of space travel. In our lifetimes, men have walked on the moon, and human travel to Mars increasingly is discussed. Talk about long-distance travel and high speed: the Apollo astronauts journeyed 250,000 miles from the earth and traveled at over 25,000 miles per hour—the fastest speeds ever achieved by human beings.

The prophecy "Many will go back and forth" predicts a dramatic increase in travel in the last days.

Another way this prophecy of travel is being fulfilled in our day is through massive increases in human migration. According to the United Nations, the number of international migrants globally was an estimated 272 million in 2019, up from 153 million in 1990 and 84 million in 1980. That's an increase of over 200 percent in just forty years. Further, the percentage of the world's population migrating each year has risen from about 2.3 percent in 1980 to 3.5 percent today—an increase of over 50 percent in just forty years.[29]

I hope I've made the case: in our day *many* are going "back and forth"—a clear fulfillment of the Daniel 12:4 prophecy.

"And Knowledge Will Increase"

The second half of Daniel 12:4—"and knowledge will increase"—fits our time just as well. We live in an era of amazing knowledge and technology that is far beyond the wildest dreams of people who lived only a few decades ago.

In his 1982 book *Critical Path*, futurist Buckminster Fuller described the "accelerating acceleration" of human knowledge and technology over time (sometimes called the "Knowledge Doubling Curve").[30] The book's appendix details a series of discoveries and innovations, demonstrating that human knowledge doubled once between 1 AD and 1500 AD—roughly the time of the invention of the printing press. (Opinions differ about who was the last person to know everything that could be known—some say Renaissance genius Sir Francis Bacon—but whoever he or she was lived about this time.)

In large part due to the invention of the printing press just before 1500, the next doubling of knowledge required only 250 years, and the next, only 150 years, meaning that by 1900 the world had eight times the accumulated knowledge it had at the time of Christ.

But Fuller observed that the rate of growth was continuing to increase. Knowledge doubled again in the fifty years between 1900 and 1950, and again in the twenty years to 1970, and yet again in just ten years ending in 1980. Today, thanks to the Internet, some estimate that the doubling time is down to less than a year, and some think it will soon be measured in hours. (Of course, knowledge increases in different fields at different rates; these numbers are illustrative averages and estimates.) If you were to graph this curve, it would look like figure 2: a classic hockey stick, virtually flat for centuries before beginning to bend up two hundred years ago and now rising almost vertically.

Figure 2: The Explosion of Knowledge in Our Day

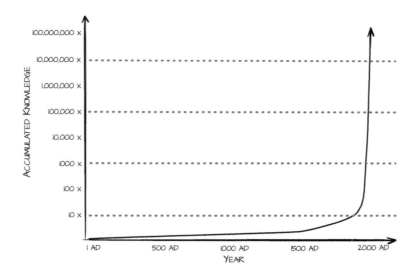

Clearly, that fits our life experience. Consider the technological innovations that have occurred just in my sixty-three-year lifetime: personal computers, cell phones, the Internet, the global positioning system, laparoscopic surgery, LASIK, CAT scans, transplant surgery, joint replacements, microwave ovens, the jet airliner, fiber optics, genetic engineering, space travel—the list goes on and on. And if you go back another sixty years, the list would include such things as television, automobiles, airplanes, antibiotics, vaccinations, and many more. Because of all of these innovations, the average person today arguably enjoys a life that even a king could not imagine 150 years ago. All are signs of the explosion of knowledge in our day.

Thanks to the invention of the Internet, all of this knowledge is available at the touch of a button to nearly everyone in the world. I sometimes tell my children how difficult it was in the old days to get your hands on an article or book you wanted to read or needed for an assignment. (I guess that's my version of "I had to walk five miles to school, through the snow, uphill—both ways!") Today, there is no need for anyone not to know whatever they want to know—it's all right there at our fingertips.

The rapid advance of communication technology opens the door for the fulfillment of the prophecy from Revelation 11:7–9 (NLT) concerning the two witnesses. After they have preached their message, "the beast that comes up out of the bottomless pit will . . . kill them. And their bodies will lie in the main street of Jerusalem . . . And for three and a half days, all peoples, tribes, languages, and nations will stare at their bodies." Before the days of television and communication satellites—and now, the Internet, computers, and smartphones—no one could have guessed how it was possible for an image to be viewed by people all over the world in real time. But today it's commonplace.

No doubt the explosion of knowledge and invention will continue at an increasing pace. And travel may become even easier and faster. Who knows what's possible? Even so, the point is that the prophecy of "Many will go back and forth, and knowledge will increase" is an amazingly accurate description of our times. If this prophecy describes the world "at the time of the end," is there any doubt that we're living in the last days—and that Jesus is coming soon?

THE GOSPEL COMES TO The Muslim World

For centuries, missiologists wondered how the Muslim world would be reached. Although many had tried, no one had been able to produce much fruit from Muslim evangelism.

But today, God is gathering an astounding harvest from among the Muslim people. For example, it is widely thought that the church in Iran—one of the world's most fundamentalist Islamic countries—is the fastest growing church in the world.

In many places the Holy Spirit is using dreams and visions to open Muslims to the gospel. These visions often involve a man in brilliant white clothing who invites the dreamer to follow him and instructs him to seek out a believer who can explain the gospel to him. Many have come to faith in this way.

The Finishing Fund has seen remarkable results in many of the projects we support targeting Muslim people groups, and those results are supported by other ministries. Global Media Outreach, an Internet-based ministry, reported in their Muslim World Report that they had received 519,741 indicated decisions for Christ from Muslim countries in just the month of August 2019. That's five hundred thousand converts from Islam in *one month* through *one ministry*! To put that in context, it is unlikely that five hundred thousand Muslims in total converted to Christianity in all the 1,400 years from the founding of Islam up to the year 2000.

The gospel is coming to the Muslim people.

8

Love Grown Cold

For the church, the days leading up to Jesus' return will be, to paraphrase Charles Dickens, the worst of times and the best of times. As his return draws near, the Bible says, the church will experience apathy and apostasy—a "great falling away"—driven by growing persecution, false teaching, and the increasing wickedness of the culture. At the same time, though, we will experience growth and great joy as we fulfill Jesus' command to "make disciples of every nation" and look forward with increasing excitement to his return.

Persecution

Matthew 24:9 prophesies that in the last days believers "will be handed over to be persecuted and put to death, and you will be hated by all nations because of me." Does this describe the state of Christianity in the 2020s? Increasingly, it does. Today, we see growing persecution of the church around the world.

According to Open Doors, which tracks persecution of Christians, in 2020 more than 340 million Christians—more than 1 of every 8 believers worldwide—lived in places where they experience high levels of persecution.[31]

A report ordered by British Foreign Secretary Jeremy Hunt found that the persecution of Christians in parts of the world is at near-genocide levels. The report says, "Evidence shows not only the geographic spread of anti-Christian persecution, but also its increasing severity" and that "in some regions, the level and nature of persecution is arguably coming close to meeting the international definition of genocide, according to that adopted by the UN.[32]

A 2017 study published by Aid to the Church in Need reports that treatment of Christians has worsened substantially in recent years and is more violent now than at any other period in modern time.[33]

In Nigeria, Christians are in a fight for survival against Boko Haram fundamentalists and Fulani herdsmen. Many have been killed and many more have been driven out of their homes in Nigeria's Northern states. Thirteen thousand churches have been closed or destroyed as a result of the violence.[34]

In China, which may be home to more than 100 million Christians, believers are increasingly targeted by the country's growing surveillance apparatus and its social credit system. Over the past year, local governments have shut (and in some cases, bulldozed) hundreds of unofficial house churches that operate outside the government-approved church network. Christians are enduring the worst crackdown since the country's Cultural Revolution, when Mao Zedong attempted to eradicate religion.

The rise of Hindu nationalism in India has resulted in increasingly violent incidents against Christians. Several states in India have adopted anti-conversion laws, which the ruling Hindu nationalist BJP party wants to apply nationwide. These laws are often used as an excuse to disrupt church services, harass Christians, and make it difficult for Christians to share their faith. Reports show that government food aid has been withheld from Christians unless they will renounce their faith.

As a result of the Syrian civil war, between 2012 and 2017 the number of Syrian Christians dropped from 1.7 million to less than 500,000.[35] In Iraq ethnic cleansing and genocide have reduced the Christian population from 1.5 million in 2003 to below 120,000. Some think that Christianity in Iraq will be wiped out completely.[36]

Today, we see growing persecution of the church around the world.

We don't see anything like this yet in the United States, although opposition to Christianity and Christians has clearly been increasing. Take the case of Jack Phillips, the Colorado baker who has been sued repeatedly over his faith-based refusal to bake cakes for same-sex marriage ceremonies. It isn't hard to imagine how conflict over cultural issues like same-sex marriage could lead to increasing legal attacks on and hostility toward churches and Christians.

Despite all this, though, I think we have barely begun to see the fulfillment of this prophecy. I expect that over the next few years, as the rapture and the tribulation draw even nearer, persecution of the church—both in the West and around the world—will increase dramatically. Jesus encourages us to endure what's coming, promising that "the one who stands firm to the end will be saved" (Matt. 24:13). Even in the face of increasing opposition and persecution, he says, we must stand firm, trusting him as our Rock, our Strong Tower, our Strength and our Shield, and using every bit of the spiritual armor with which he has equipped us.

Persecution of the Jews

It's important to remember that the disciples were Jews before they were Christians, so when Jesus spoke to them about persecution in the last days, I think he wasn't just describing the persecution of the church, but also increasing persecution of the Jews.

Do we see that today? We do. Increasing oppression to the Jews in nineteenth-century Europe, particularly in Russia, was one of the drivers for the Zionist movement and the establishment of modern Israel. And in probably the most horrific example of religious persecution in the history of the world, six million Jews were killed in the Holocaust in the 1930s and 1940s. We also see persecution of the Jews in the continual opposition to Israel in the world community, especially among many of the world's Muslim countries.

A survey published by the American Jewish Committee revealed that more than 80 percent of respondents say they have witnessed an increase in anti-Semitic incidents in the United States over the past five years. Forty-three percent say the increase has been significant. Likewise, the Anti-Defamation League reported a 150 percent increase in recorded incidents of anti-Semitism in 2018 compared to 2013.[37]

The same is true across Europe. In England the Community Security Trust recorded 1,805 antisemitic incidents in 2019, the highest number ever logged and a 7 percent increase from 2018.[38] In Germany anti-Semitic crimes, including hate speech, rose by 20 percent in 2018, and there were sixty-two violent anti-Semitic attacks, compared to thirty-seven in 2017. The government has advised the few Jews remaining in the country against wearing the kippa, or yarmulke.[39] According to France's National Human Rights Advisory Committee (CNCDH), in 2018 anti-Semitic acts in France increased more than 70 percent compared to the previous year. Thousands of Jews have left Paris over the last few years to escape these attacks.[40]

I would expect the frequency and intensity of Jewish persecution to increase as the day of Jesus' return draws near—especially after the rapture occurs. As a result, more and more Jews will make *aliyah*, or emigrating to Israel, setting the stage for the coming of the antichrist and the tribulation.

False Prophets

In Matthew 24:11, Jesus warns us that in the last days, "many false prophets will appear and deceive many people." First Timothy 4:1–3 supports this prophecy:

> The Spirit clearly says that in later times some will abandon the faith and follow deceiving spirits and things taught by demons. Such teachings come through hypocritical liars, whose consciences have been seared as with a hot iron.

Later in Matthew 24, Jesus warns that the number and influence of these false messiahs and false prophets will multiply as the Day of

Christ draws nearer. These imposters will "perform great signs and wonders to deceive, if possible, even the elect" (v. 24).

In 2 Corinthians 11:13 Paul warns about these frauds, saying, "Such people are false apostles, deceitful workers, masquerading as apostles of Christ." We see much the same thing in 2 Peter 2.

We tend to think of these false teachers as being associated with cults—the Mormons, Jehovah's Witnesses, Moonies, or Shincheonji—or TV preachers with sketchy doctrine. It's true that false teachers like these have misled their share of the undiscerning.

But another fulfillment of this prophecy would include the theologians in the "higher criticism" movement of the nineteenth and early twentieth centuries. These scholars used literary and historical techniques to attack and undermine the historicity and authority of the Scriptures, arguing, for example, that Moses did not write the Pentateuch and that the exodus never took place. The result was that many lost confidence in the Bible as the authoritative word of God, with predictable results. Much of modern liberal Protestantism is anchored in this school of theology.

Attacks from the Outside

In my opinion, though, the most damaging and insidious "false prophets" of our era are those who have attacked the church from the outside. These antireligious false teachers are deceiving millions—many more, I think, than all the cults combined.

DARWIN, MARX, AND FREUD

Think about the famous late-nineteenth- and early-twentieth-century "false prophets" Charles Darwin, Karl Marx, and Sigmund Freud.

Each promoted ideas that undermined orthodox Christianity and advanced materialistic and humanistic philosophies. Darwin famously proposed a materialistic explanation for the diversity of life in the world—evolution as a result of natural selection—that undermined the idea of God as the creator of all life. Marx reduced life to a materialistic struggle for economic power and dismissed religion as the "opiate of the masses." In books such as *Totem and Taboo*, *Moses and Monotheism*, and *The Future of an Illusion*, Freud shriveled religion to nothing more than a set of superstitions invented by the ancients to cope with inexplicable natural phenomena and deep-seated psychological distress.

> *The most damaging "false prophets" are those who have attacked the church from the outside.*

THE NEW ATHEISTS

In our day, "new atheist" teachers including Sam Harris, Christopher Hitchens, Richard Dawkins, and Daniel Dennett (the so-called Four Horsemen of Atheism), Bart Ehrman, and Carl Sagan fervently oppose Christianity. The titles of their books say everything you need to know about them: Dawkins' *The God Delusion*, Hitchens's *God Is Not Great*, Harris's *The End of Faith*, and Ehrman's *How Jesus Became God*. Carl Sagan is famous for his blasphemous (and transparently false) assertion that "the Cosmos is all that is or was or ever will be."[41]

In this same camp are the many university professors who preach atheism, socialism, critical race theory, and other lies to credulous college students. How many young people enter university each year as Christians and return home for Thanksgiving as atheists, the victims of these false teachers?

Moral Rebels

A similar class of false teachers are those who promote transgressive moral agendas, including abortion, homosexuality, and transgenderism. For example, Margaret Sanger, the eugenicist founder of Planned Parenthood, was an early and influential advocate for abortion and even infanticide. In her book *Woman and the New Race*, she wrote, "The most merciful thing that the large family does to one of its infant members is to kill it."[42] Most of these false teachers are not personally as well-known as the atheists, but their thinking has been amplified by the media and now pervades our culture.

Environmentalism

A fourth group of false prophets are the radical environmentalists. In our day environmentalism has become, in effect, a new post-Christian pagan religion, worshipping the planet, which some have named Gaia. Here's what author Michael Crichton says about environmentalism as a new religion:

> There's an initial Eden, a paradise, a state of grace and unity with nature, there's a fall from grace into a state of pollution as a result of eating from the tree of knowledge, and as a result of our actions there is a judgment day coming for us all. We are all energy sinners, doomed to die, unless we seek salvation, which is now called sustainability. Sustainability is salvation in the church of the environment. Just

as organic food is its communion, that pesticide-free wafer that the right people with the right beliefs, imbibe.[43]

Freeman Dyson, the famous physicist, has described environmentalism as "a worldwide secular religion" that has "replaced socialism as the leading secular religion." It holds "that we are stewards of the earth, that despoiling the planet with waste products of our luxurious living is a sin, and that the path of righteousness is to live as frugally as possible."[44]

The radical environmental movement is neopagan—a return to the ancient fertility religions that worshipped the earth. And it is exactly what Paul describes in Romans 1:25 when he speaks of those who have "exchanged the truth about God for a lie, and worshiped and served created things rather than the Creator."

Environmentalism has become, in effect, a new post-Christian pagan religion

(Just so you'll know, I am a conservationist. For the last nine years I've been rehabilitating a rural property near my home—a former cattle farm—replacing over one hundred acres of fescue with native prairie grasses and wildflowers and planting over thirty thousand seedling trees. As a Christian, I believe in protecting and preserving nature. But I don't believe that nature is to be worshipped or that environmental stewardship is a path to righteousness.)

An Epidemic among the Young

Sadly, the ideas promoted by these false prophets have led many people away from the Christian faith. Young people in particular seem to be vulnerable to their influence. We see this in our own family, where one of our grown children has become an atheist after growing up in the church, and we see it in the families of many of our friends. Just in our Sunday school class of perhaps fifty couples, at least ten have children who are pursuing atheism and/or same-sex relationships. It's like an epidemic among the young brought about by false teachers.

Scoffers

As we get closer to the second coming, we will see more people expressing doubt about Jesus—both his existence and his return. Second Peter 3:3–7 predicts:

> Above all, you must understand that in the last days scoff-
> ers will come, scoffing and following their own evil desires.
> They will say, "Where is this 'coming' he promised? Ever
> since our ancestors died, everything goes on as it has since
> the beginning of creation." But they deliberately forget
> that long ago by God's word the heavens came into being
> and the earth was formed out of water and by water. By
> these waters also the world of that time was deluged and
> destroyed. By the same word the present heavens and earth
> are reserved for fire, being kept for the day of judgment
> and destruction of the ungodly.

Doesn't this perfectly describe the atheistic, uniformitarian world-view that dominates the West today? According to Peter, these scoffers "deliberately" ignore the truth of God's creation and judg-ment so that they can follow "their own evil desires." They also mock those who are looking for the return of Christ: "Where is this 'coming' he promised?" But Peter concludes, "But the day of the Lord will come." It certainly will.

A Form of Godliness

Paul describes the character of these false prophets in 2 Timothy 3:1–5. We don't have room here to consider all of the accusations Paul makes about these people. Suffice to say that he's describing complete moral failing: these people will be selfish, proud, undisciplined, decadent, and more. Sadly, we all can think of examples of this kind of behavior inside the church. And of course, these things are even more descriptive of many of those attacking and undermining the faith from the outside.

I'm particularly intrigued by what Paul says in 2 Timothy 3:5— that these people will have "a form of godliness but denying its power"—and verse 8, "these teachers oppose the truth." To me, this brings to mind so many teachers in liberal churches who occupy pulpits, preach sermons, administer the sacraments, and deliver benedictions—that's "a form of godliness"—but don't really believe the Bible and its teaching— that's "denying its power." Instead of

> *Paul describes the false teachers as having "a form of godliness but denying its power."*

preaching the truth of the Bible (which they do not believe is true), they preach a progressive agenda of social justice. Many don't really believe in the gospel—which, interestingly, Paul describes in 1 Corinthians 1:18 as "the power of God"—because they don't really believe that people are sinners in need of salvation. Few would know of the dynamic power of the Spirit-filled life. Some might even deny that Jesus was a real person. Just think of the churches and even entire denominations that embrace same-sex marriage, or churches that deny the truth of the creation, the exodus, miracles, the resurrection, and the return of Christ.

And what better describes the prophets of the new atheism than "these teachers oppose the truth" (2 Tim. 3:1–5)? Their entire purpose is to stand against God and his truth.

The Ultimate Fulfillment

Ultimately, this prophecy will be fulfilled during the tribulation by the "second beast" of Revelation 13. This "false prophet" will perform "great signs," including calling fire from heaven to prove the antichrist's claim to deity, thus mimicking the miracle God performed through Elijah at Mount Carmel. And he will require that "the earth and its inhabitants worship the first beast" (Rev. 13:12). For a time, he will be allowed to deceive the entire planet. But then Jesus will return and sweep him away with a word.

Falling Away

Sadly, the Bible repeatedly predicts that in the days before Jesus returns there will be a great falling away from the faith—an endtimes apostasy—as a result of increasing persecution, false teaching, and the growing wickedness of culture. In 1 Timothy, Paul predicts that "many will abandon the faith." In 2 Thessalonians 2, he predicts a "rebellion" in the culture and the church. And Jesus himself warned that the love of many people toward God and the church would "grow cold."

Let's explore these prophecies and consider whether we see signs of them being fulfilled in our day.

Abandoning the Faith

First Timothy 4:1 warns, "The Spirit clearly says that in later times some will abandon the faith and follow deceiving spirits and things taught by demons."

We've already considered how many in our culture have been deceived by the false teachings of materialism, humanism, and environmentalism and how this has caused many to abandon the faith. Whether ideas like Darwinism are "things taught by demons," certainly the aggressive new atheist movement fits that description. And the mass exodus from the faith of the young adult children of faithful Christians feels like a demonic delusion—an evil spiritual wind sweeping away our kids.

Recently, a flurry of Christian celebrities—musicians, authors, Internet personalities, and even pastors—have publicly declared that they are no longer believers or that they have embraced heretical doctrines. Joshua Harris, author of the influential book *I Kissed Dating Goodbye*, announced in 2019, "By all the measurements that I have for defining a Christian, I am not a Christian."[45] Marty Sampson, a leader of the Hillsong worship music team,

> *The Bible repeatedly predicts that there will be a great falling away from the faith before Jesus returns.*

proclaimed on Instagram that "I'm genuinely losing my faith. . . . I am not in anymore. I want genuine truth. . . . Christianity just seems to me like another religion at this point."[46] And in 2016 popular author and speaker Jen Hatmaker announced her support for same-sex marriage—a position affirmed by her husband, pastor Brandon Hatmaker: "We both believe a same-sex marriage, as a life-long monogamous commitment, can be holy before God."[47]

Sadly, because of the influence of these leaders and others like them, many are being misled and deceived.

The Rebellion

In 2 Thessalonians 2:3 Paul prophesies a coming rebellion against God: "That day will not come until the rebellion occurs and the man of lawlessness is revealed, the man doomed to destruction." The Greek word translated "rebellion" by the NIV is *apostasia*, and while rebellion is an acceptable translation, I wonder why the translators didn't just use the English word *apostasy*, abandonment of one's religious faith. Paul describes here the same thing he predicted in 1 Timothy 4 and what Jesus prophesies in Matthew 24: a great falling away from the faith in the last days.

Love Grown Cold

Matthew 24:10–13 warns,

> At that time *many will turn away from the faith* and will betray and hate each other . . . Because of the increase of wickedness, *the love of most will grow cold*, but the one who stands firm to the end will be saved.

Again, we see the prediction of a falling away in the last days. Jesus says, "Many will turn away from the faith" and "the love of most will grow cold."

It seems clear that "many" and "most" describe at least nominal believers. Turning away from the faith implies that one had once turned toward it, and love growing cold implies that it had once been warmer. Those who are falling away must have had at least some level of connection with Christianity.

What does Jesus mean by "the love of most will grow cold?" Love toward whom? In context, I think the best answer is "toward God." The Bible teaches that we show love toward God through our obedience to his commands. Jesus taught, "If you love me, keep my commands" (John 14:15) and "If you keep my commands, you will remain in my love, just as I have kept my Father's commands and remain in his love" (John 15:10). If we show love toward God through obedience, then "the love of most will grow cold" is a prediction of widespread disobedience in the last days—a falling away.

Instead of loving God, in the last days people will love themselves, as we saw in 2 Timothy 3:1, and the world, as explained in 1 John 2:15: "If anyone loves the world, love for the Father is not in them."

This disobedience toward God will also result in the love of many toward one another growing cold. Jesus predicts that as well when he says "many . . . will betray and hate each other." My guess is that we'll see more and more of this kind of behavior as persecution intensifies and people increasingly seek to protect themselves instead of loving and caring for others.

Increasing Wickedness

Why will this happen? Jesus says it will be due to "the increase of wickedness" in the days before his return. In the previous chapter we saw how we are living out Jesus' prophecy that in the last days the world will be like the days of Noah and the days of Lot: filled with increasing wickedness.

Sadly, though, Jesus predicts here that in the last days the wickedness of *culture* will infect and corrupt the *church*. And of course, we see that vividly today as well. Surveys indicate that across a wide range of behaviors—premarital sex, gambling, divorce, drug use, pornography—there is little difference between the behavior of churched Americans and the unchurched. In their book *unChristian*, authors David Kinnaman and Gabe Lyons write, "In virtually every study we conducted, representing thousands of interviews, born-again Christians fail to display much attitudinal or behavioral evidence of transformed lives." Kinnaman concludes, "Our lives don't match our beliefs. In many ways, our lifestyles and perspectives are no different from those of anyone around us."[48] Researcher George Barna agrees, saying "One of the greatest frustrations of my life has been the disconnection between what our research consistently shows about churched Christians and what the Bible calls us to be."[49]

By the Numbers

Some think the great apostasy will be a gradual falling away, while others think this will be a definitive event—a specific moment at which the church turns away from Christ and his commands. But whether there will be a defining act of rebellion in the future, we clearly already see an accelerating falling away from the church in the West.

According to the book *Churchless* by Barna Research, 65 percent of Americans qualify as moderately to highly post-Christian in their worldview. Almost half the US population is unchurched, up from

20 percent in the early 1990s, and 20 percent of the unchurched would consider themselves to be atheists and agnostics. Barna adds, "More than one third of America's adults are essentially secular in belief and practice. If nothing else, this helps explain why America has experienced a surge in unchurched people."[50]

The falling away is most pronounced among young people. According to Gallup, only 42 percent of American millennials attend church.[51] A survey by Rainer Research reveals that about 70 percent of America's young people drop out of church between the ages of eighteen and twenty-two.[52] At the 2009 Pew Forum on Religion and Public Life, political scientists Robert Putnam and David Campbell reported that "young Americans are dropping out of religion at an alarming rate of *five to six times* the historic rate."[53] Barna reports that 60 percent of today's young adults in their 20s who attended church during their teen years are "spiritually disengaged."[54]

Jesus predicts that in the last days the wickedness of culture will infect the church.

In her 2008 book *Quitting Church*, Julia Duin writes: "It's no secret that the percentage of Americans in church on any given Sunday is dropping fast." She contends that only about 4 percent of young people will end up attending church as adults, compared to 35 percent of baby boomers and 65 percent of the World War II–era "Greatest Generation."[55]

But There Is Also Joy

Well, that sounds great, doesn't it? Persecution, heresy, wickedness, and apostasy, all likely to increase in the coming years. It's enough to make you wish for the return of Christ—and fortunately, that's exactly what's about to happen.

It's interesting that the paragraph in Matthew 24 that promises growing persecution, wickedness, and apostasy ends with the promise of verse 14: "This gospel of the kingdom will be preached in the whole word as a testimony to all nations, and then the end will come."

At the very time the church is experiencing swelling opposition, the gospel will finally be reaching "the ends of the earth," opening the door to Jesus' return. Millions are being added to the church from the Muslim, Hindu, and Buddhist religions and from people groups around the world where there had never before been even one Jesus follower. We're witnessing that very thing today. It may seem that God's Spirit is withdrawing from the West, but he is moving with great power in many other parts of the world, gathering in a great end-times harvest.

So even as our lives are getting tougher, we're experiencing joy as we see the final victory drawing near and anticipation for our "blessed hope"—the soon return of our Lord Jesus!

Two Questions,
Two Answers

The Olivet Discourse, recorded in Luke 21, Matthew 24, and Mark 13, is an important source of prophecy about the return of Christ. We've already considered Matthew 24 extensively throughout this book. In this chapter, though, we're going to run through that chapter, and its parallel, Luke 21, one more time to explain the order and significance of the various signs Jesus describes.

I've saved this chapter to near the end because, although it explains important prophecies, these prophecies are not particularly helpful for predicting the timing of Jesus' return. As we'll see, some of the prophecies in Luke 21 and Matthew 24 describe events that are not really signs of his return but that have been common throughout human history. Jesus mentions them because he does not want us to misunderstand them when they occur as signs of his imminent return. Other prophecies from these chapters predict events that will take place during the tribulation, by which time it will be evident that the end is here. They describe the events of the end times, but by the time they occur, there will be no doubt that the day of God is at hand.

Two Questions

The discourse in both Luke 21 and Matthew 24 begins with the disciples admiring the temple, and in both chapters Jesus responds by telling them that it will be destroyed: that "the time will come when not one stone will be left on another; every one of them will be thrown down" (Luke 21:6). In Matthew's account, the disciples, stunned by Jesus' prophecy, ask him, "When will this happen, and what will be the sign of your coming and of the end of the age?" (Matt. 24:3)

Since the disciples asked two questions, Jesus gives two answers.

To fully understand Jesus' answer to this question, we have to see that the disciples asked not one but two questions: First, when will the temple be destroyed? And second, when are you coming back to end the age and establish your kingdom? (The disciples probably thought that the two questions were one and the same, which is why they asked them together.)

Since they asked two questions, Jesus gives two answers. Some of the events he describes in Matthew 24 apply to one event—the destruction of the temple—and some to the other—his return and the end of the age. Because these answers are interwoven, it can be hard to draw out which parts of Jesus' answer apply to which question.

Although Luke records the disciples' questions differently, the same thing applies to his account in Luke 21. Some of what Jesus describes in that chapter applies to one question—when will the temple be destroyed?—and some to the second question—when are you coming back?

Table 2: Harmony of Luke 21 and Matthew 24

Luke 21	Matthew 24	Event
v. 5	v. 1	Disciples admire temple
v. 6	v. 2	Jesus prophesies destruction
v. 7	v. 3	Disciples' question(s)
vv. 8–11	vv. 4–8	Precursory signs/beginning of birth pangs
	vv. 9–13	End of the age
	v. 14	End of the age
vv. 12–24	vv. 15–20	70 AD/temple's destruction
vv. 25–27	vv. 21–30	End of the age
vv. 29–32	vv. 32–33	Parable of the Fig Tree
v. 33	v. 34	Both 70 AD and end of the age

That's confusing, but it's not unusual for biblical prophecy. As we saw in chapter 1, some of the Old Testament prophecies about

Jesus speak of both his first and second coming—sometimes in the same sentence! I think God does this for the same reason Jesus sometimes taught in parables: to deliberately veil the truth so that it is only available to his people though the revelatory power of the Holy Spirit. At first, Jesus' answer can seem confusing and contradictory, but when we think it through with the guidance of the Spirit, it becomes clear and understandable.

Thankfully, Luke provides some clues in his version that help us figure out what part of Jesus' answer applies to what part of the disciples' question.

The Precursory Signs

In Luke 21:8–11, Jesus says,

> "Watch out that you are not deceived. For many will come in my name, claiming, 'I am he,' and, 'The time is near.' Do not follow them. When you hear of wars and uprisings, do not be frightened. These things must happen first, but the end will not come right away."

> Then he said to them: "Nation will rise against nation, and kingdom against kingdom. There will be great earthquakes, famines and pestilences in various places, and fearful events and great signs from heaven."

We might call these the various signs mentioned in this passage "precursory signs" because, as Jesus says in verse 9b, "These things must happen first, but the end will not come right away." In other words, Jesus is saying that these things—false messiahs, wars,

famines, disease, and heavenly signs—should not be miscon-
strued as signs that his return is imminent. Instead, they describe
events that have been present at all times throughout human history. They may increase in frequency and severity as the last days
approach, but even so they are not specifically signs that he is
coming soon.

Matthew describes these precursory signs as "the beginnings
of the birth pangs"—in other words, signs that will precede the
events of his actual coming. As I'm writing this, my daughter-
in-law is about to give birth to our second grandson. Several
days ago, she began to experience some initial contractions, and
my wife and I got excited. But it's now three days later and still
not much has happened. Is our grandson coming soon? Yes.
But is he coming today? Probably not. Those initial birth pangs
were only precursors to his arrival, not the announcement of his
imminent birth.

False Messiahs

Religious heretics and false messiahs have been around as long as
the church. If you don't believe me, just look at the Wikipedia article titled "List of messiah claimants." I had no idea!

As we'll see a little later, Matthew 24:23–28 predicts a sharp
increase in false messiahs during the time of the tribulation, after
Jesus has raptured his church.

Wars

Similarly, while there is some evidence that wars may have increased
in the twentieth and twenty-first centuries—it's certainly true that

before the twentieth century there had never been global wars such as World War I and World War II—wars have been a constant (and horrible) part of civilization from Jesus' day. There is nothing new about the prevalence of war in the world.

Famine and Disease

Likewise, famine and disease have been part of the human experience since the fall. And instead of increasing in our lifetimes, both have decreased dramatically in the twentieth century. Famine has declined as a result of increasing freedom and prosperity, and disease has decreased thanks to invention of vaccinations and antibiotics and improvements in health care. Diseases such as smallpox and polio that once ravaged the world have been eradicated.

Interestingly, though, 2020 saw the first worldwide pestilence of our generation, COVID-19. As a result of the widespread lockdowns imposed in an effort to control COVID, experts fear that perhaps 130 million people worldwide are at risk of starvation. Remember: in many parts of the world, if you don't work today, you don't eat tonight—and people cannot work when they are confined to their homes. At the same time, natural disasters, including floods and locust plagues (that sounds biblical, right?) have been occurring around the world. Consider these stories from an email I received recently from a mission organization I respect:

Some prophecies in Luke 21 and Matthew 24 describe events that have been common throughout history.

Sudan: "We had to eat our seeds for planting"
. . . 10m facing food shortages

Ethiopia: A second generation of locusts is invading
. . . one million people will likely need emergency food
assistance
. . . worst locust infestation in Ethiopia in twenty-five years

Yemen: 2020 could be worst year yet for hunger in Yemen.
. . . half the country relying on food aid to survive
. . . "perfect storm" of war, COVID-19, floods, locusts

Bangladesh: A quarter submerged, millions lose everything.
. . . torrential rains follow cyclone two months ago
. . . pattern of more severe, more frequent river flooding
. . . "severe food related distress because of the pandemic."

Could it be that we are witnessing a return to the biblical pattern?

Heavenly Signs

Last but not least, heavenly signs such as eclipses, comets, and meteor showers have been present from the creation through the present and have often been regarded, among Christians and pagans alike, as signs of looming apocalypse. Tremendous energy has been invested in trying to link recent astronomical events—such as the tetrad of lunar eclipses a few years ago—to the return of Christ, but I've not heard of any credible connection.

Importantly, the heavens will show signs near the end of the tribulation that *do* signal the return of Christ. We'll consider those later.

A Different Answer

In Luke 21:12, Jesus says, "But before all this . . ." That's a signal that what follows does not continue the preceding line of thought. Jesus has been talking about one thing—the precursory signs—but now he's going to talk about another: the events that would herald the fall of Jerusalem and the destruction of the temple.

For this reason, we should regard Luke 21:12–24 as a long parenthetical in which Jesus addresses the disciples' first question: When will the temple be destroyed?

First, he says, they will be subject to extreme persecution: Jesus says, "They will hand you over to synagogues and put you in prison, and you will be brought before kings and governors" (v. 12); that they will be "betrayed even by parents, brothers and sisters, relatives and friends, and they will put some of you to death" (v. 16); and that "everyone will hate you because of me" (v. 17). That's awful, and it precisely describes what the disciples experienced. We read about some of that in Acts, and we know from history that all the apostles but John were martyred in the years *before* the destruction of Jerusalem—beginning with James in Acts 12.

As we've said already, sometimes biblical prophecies can have multiple fulfillments. That seems to be true of this prophecy of persecution: it applied once to the disciples who heard Jesus speak these words but will also be true for believers in general in the last days. We considered that sign of Jesus' return in chapter 8.

Jesus warns the disciples of coming persecution, and then he describes the days just prior to the destruction of Jerusalem. In Luke 21:20–24 he says, "When [they] see Jerusalem surrounded by armies," people should get out of the city and "flee to the

mountains." He says, "This is the time of punishment in fulfillment of all that has been written," almost certainly speaking of the
punishment prophesied in Deuteronomy 28:58. He prophesies
that the Jews "will be taken as prisoners to all the nations"—again,
a direct link to the promise of Deuteronomy 28:64 that "the LORD
will scatter you among all nations, from one end of the earth to
the other . . ."

Finally, he says, "Jerusalem will be trampled on by the Gentiles until the times of the Gentiles are fulfilled" (Luke 21:24). The
times of the gentiles began in AD 70 when the Romans destroyed
Jerusalem and expelled the Jews from their homeland, and continued through the modern era, when finally, in the twentieth century,
the Jews began to return. In 1948, when the nation of Israel officially came into existence (or perhaps in 1967, when Israel recap-
tured Jerusalem), the "times of the Gentiles" came to an end. We
examined the prophecies of scattering and regathering, and their
implications for the timing of the return of Christ, in chapter 4.

The Last Days

When Jesus says, "Jerusalem will be trampled on by the Gentiles
until the times of the Gentiles are fulfilled," he signals another shift
in time and focus, from 70 AD to our day and from the destruction
of Jerusalem to the "end of the age." So as we read Luke 21:25–28,
we should understand that the events Jesus describes are signs of his
second coming. Here's what he says:

> "There will be signs in the sun, moon and stars. On the
> earth, nations will be in anguish and perplexity at the roar-
> ing and tossing of the sea. People will faint from terror,

apprehensive of what is coming on the world, for the heavenly bodies will be shaken. At that time they will see the Son of Man coming in a cloud with power and great glory."

Let's take a look at each of these prophecies.

Signs in the Heavens

Earlier, Jesus said that "fearful events and great signs from heaven" were only precursory signs, but now he mentions them again, saying that in the time of his return there will be "signs in the sun, moon and stars" and that "the heavenly bodies will be shaken." We can only guess what they will be, although we have clues. For instance, Revelation 8:12 says, "The fourth angel sounded his trumpet, and a third of the sun was struck, a third of the moon, and a third of the stars, so that a third of them turned dark."

From the parallel passage in Matthew 24, we know that these events will take place at the end of the great tribulation, just before Jesus returns once and for all.

The Tossing of the Sea

Jesus says, "On the earth, nations will be in anguish and perplexity at the roaring and tossing of the sea" (Luke 21:25). It's possible that Jesus has in mind here a natural sign such as hurricanes or perhaps tsunamis resulting from earthquakes. But more likely, I think he's describing a time of severe worldwide social and political unrest.

Recall that in Hebrew prophecy "the sea" is symbolic of the gentile world. For example, Daniel 7 describes Daniel's dream of four beasts that "came up out of the sea," representing four successive gentile empires. So when Jesus says, "Nations will be in anguish and perplexity at the roaring and tossing of the sea," he's speaking of a time of great worldwide turmoil.

In all likelihood, Jesus is describing happenings that are still in the future—a worldwide calamity that sets the stage for the rise of the antichrist or the actual events of the tribulation. Still, the worldwide panic over COVID-19 gives us at least a sense of the state Jesus was describing. Certainly, "nations will be in anguish and perplexity" is an apt description of the world's response to COVID.

When Jesus says "the roaring and tossing of the sea," he's speaking of a time of great worldwide turmoil.

Fainting with Terror

In Luke 21:26, Jesus says, "People will faint from terror, apprehensive of what is coming on the world, for the heavenly bodies will be shaken." This verse builds on and reinforces verse 25, describing the emotions that will result from the developments in both the heavens and on the earth: terror and apprehension. Again, what exactly is meant by "heavenly bodies will be shaken" is not clear, although some link this prophecy to Revelation 6:12–14:

The sun turned black like sackcloth made of goat hair, the whole moon turned blood red, and the stars in the sky fell to earth, as figs drop from a fig tree when shaken by a strong wind. The heavens receded like a scroll being rolled up . . .

Whatever that means exactly, Jesus is clearly saying that the later days of the tribulation, immediately before his final return, will be filled with fear and dread.

Matthew 24

Matthew 24 records the same discourse found in Luke 21, although Matthew's version is not as easily dissected as Luke's. Like Luke, Matthew describes the precursory signs in verses 4 through 8, then shifts to persecution in verses 9 through 13. He says,

> "Then you will be handed over to be persecuted and put to death, and you will be hated by all nations because of me. At that time many will turn away from the faith and will betray and hate each other, and many false prophets will appear and deceive many people. Because of the increase of wickedness, the love of most will grow cold, but the one who stands firm to the end will be saved."

It's not clear whether these verses are speaking of the days before the destruction of the temple in AD 70 or the last days—or perhaps both. I think he's talking primarily about the time before his return. As we saw in chapter 8, this is just one of several prophecies of apostasy and corruption in the church in the last days.

But clearly verse 14 is speaking of the last days: "And this gospel of the kingdom will be preached in the whole world as a testimony to all nations, and then the end will come." We considered this prophecy and its implications for Jesus' imminent return in chapter 3.

The Abomination

In verses 15 and 16, Jesus warns, "When you see standing in the holy place 'the abomination that causes desolation,' spoken of through the prophet Daniel—let the reader understand—then let those who are in Judea flee to the mountains." In chapter 5, we discussed the prophecy of the abomination of desolation, which appears in Daniel 9, 11, and 12. There have been several different fulfillments of the prophecy of an "abomination that causes desolation" being set up in or on the site of the temple (and there will be one more). In this case, Jesus is probably describing the golden Roman eagle Titus erected over the temple gates in 70 AD, immediately before he destroyed both the temple and the city.

If that's correct, then like Luke, Matthew has shifted back to speaking about the events surrounding the destruction of the temple. And like Luke, he warns, "Let those who are in Judea flee to the mountains. Let no one on the housetop go down to take anything out of the house. Let no one in the field go back to get their cloak" (24:16–18). He's describing the hardships that will accompany the Roman invasion of Judea.

Time of Great Distress

In verse 21, Jesus turns again to speaking about the end times, describing "great distress, unequaled from the beginning of the world until now—and never to be equaled again." As bad as the conquest of Jerusalem in 70 AD was for the Jewish people, it certainly was no worse than what the Babylonians did to the city hundreds of years before or, for that matter, many other similar events in the history of the world since then. So when Jesus says "unequaled from the beginning of the world until now," he has to be describing the tribulation, doesn't he? Notice that Jesus' words echo the angel in Daniel 12:1, "At that time . . . There will be a time of distress such as has not happened from the beginning of nations until then." Since Daniel 12 unquestionably speaks of the end times, it makes sense to understand Jesus to be speaking about the same thing in verse 21.

> *The great tribulation will be so horrific that if God did not relent, no living thing would survive.*

Jesus continues, "If those days had not been cut short, no one would survive, but for the sake of the elect those days will be shortened" (Matt. 24:22). The great tribulation will be so horrific that if God did not relent from his judgment, no living thing would survive. Jesus says God's mercy will be "for the sake of the elect."

As I've mentioned throughout this book, I believe that the church—the "elect"—will not be required to suffer through the tribulation but will be raptured out of the world before it begins. So who are the "elect" in verse 22? They must be those who have come to faith after the rapture, during the tribulation. Sadly, these brothers and sisters (those who are not martyred) will be left in the world during the tribulation and will suffer through its judgments. But mercifully, God will "cut short" the days of judgment for their sake.

False Messiahs

Earlier, I said that false messiahs have been common throughout history, both before and after Jesus, and for that reason that we shouldn't consider any particular false messiah to be a sign of Jesus' return. But then in Matthew 24:23–28 Jesus speaks at length about "false messiahs and false prophets" who will appear "at that time"— during the time of "great distress" described in Matthew 24:21. He warns us not to believe those who tell us of mysterious, secret messiahs "out in the wilderness" or "in the inner rooms."

Evidently, the distress of the great tribulation will cause many to seek out saviors and many others to pretend to meet their need for comfort. But, Jesus says, you won't have to guess about whether he's come back. No, he says, there will not be anything hidden or secretive about his final coming: "For as lightning that comes from the east is visible even in the west, so will be the coming of the Son of Man" (Matt. 24:27).

Then Will Appear the Son of Man

Finally, Jesus says in verses 29 and 30, "Immediately after the distress of those days, 'the sun will be darkened, and the moon will not give its light; the stars will fall from the sky, and the heavenly bodies will be shaken.' Then will appear the sign of the Son of Man in heaven."

"Immediately after the distress of those days" places these events at the very end of the tribulation, just before the return of Jesus. Notice the direct parallel to Luke 21:25–27: "There will be signs in the sun, moon and stars. . . . for the heavenly bodies will be shaken. At that time they will see the Son of Man coming in a cloud with power and great glory." Both passages describe great astronomical signs that will immediately precede the return of Christ.

The Fig Tree

In both Luke 21 and Matthew 24, Jesus wraps up his discourse by telling the Parable of the Fig Tree. Matthew 24:32–34 says,

> "Now learn this lesson from the fig tree: As soon as its twigs get tender and its leaves come out, you know that summer is near. Even so, when you see all these things, you know that it is near, right at the door. Truly I tell you, this generation will certainly not pass away until all these things have happened."

Verses 32 and 33 are often cited as a prophecy of the reestablishment of the nation of Israel before the return of Christ, as we saw in chapter 4. So those verses apparently are part of the answer to the question "When are you coming back?"

But then in verse 34, Jesus says that "this generation will certainly not pass away until all these things have happened." Is Jesus saying that his disciples would live to see his return? If so, we're got a real problem, since all of them—even John, who lived the longest—have been dead for millennia.

Jesus said that "this generation will certainly not pass away until all these things have happened."

When Jesus says, "This generation will certainly not pass away until all these things have happened," he almost certainly was speaking about two different generations and two different sets of events. Remember, Jesus is answering two questions in Matthew 24 and Luke 21:

"When will the temple be destroyed?" and "When are you coming back?" This one verse actually is part of both answers.

With regard to the question "When will the temple be destroyed?," when Jesus says, "This generation will certainly not pass away until all these things have happened," he's speaking about the disciples and he's saying that their generation will witness the temple's destruction. That prophecy was fulfilled in 70 AD when the Romans destroyed Jerusalem—within the expected lifetimes of most of the disciples.

But as we saw in chapter 4, if Jesus is answering the disciples' second question, "this generation" describes those who witness the regathering of Israel—the greening of the fig tree—and "all these things" would describe the signs of his return.

That's confusing, but remember what we said at the start of this chapter: In biblical prophecy, sometimes one statement can refer to more than one event. Matthew 24:34 is an excellent example of that phenomenon.

Conclusion

Often, you'll hear people talking about escalating war and various events in nature—famines, earthquakes, eclipses, and the like—as signs of the end of the age. But Jesus actually taught that things like these would take place all through history and were at best the "beginning of the birth pangs" preceding his return.

What's more, as we study Luke 21 and Matthew 24, we must keep in mind that those chapters answer not just one question—"When are you coming back?"—but a second question as well: "When will the temple be destroyed?" If we miss that, we'll get confused as Jesus bounces back and forth between one answer and the other.

And last, we have to see that some of the prophecies in these chapters concern events that will take place during the great tribulation, after the rapture, when there will be no doubt that his return is near.

Fortunately, the Bible contains other clues that *do* help us know we are living in the days of Jesus' return, including the key prophecy from Matthew 24:14: "And this gospel of the kingdom will be preached in the whole world as a testimony to all nations, and then the end will come." And since we're close to that goal, his return is closer every day. He's coming soon.

10

Only the Father

When people say that we cannot know when Jesus is coming back, they often point to his own words in Matthew 24:36: "But about that day or hour no one knows, not even the angels in heaven, nor the Son, but only the Father." In fact, this may be the best-known verse in all the Bible concerning the return of Christ. And sadly, it discourages many from exploring what the Bible teaches about when Jesus will return. If we can't know, why bother asking?

But what if this verse—far from discouraging us against exploring the timing of Jesus' return—is actually a massive hint about the timing of his return? What if it actually points to one of the seven God-ordained feasts—the Feast of Trumpets—and thus to the exact time of year he will come back?

We'll get to that, but first we need to do a survey of the seven feasts of Israel and how Jesus has fulfilled—or will fulfill—each of them.[56]

The Feasts of Israel

God gave the feasts of Israel to the nation through Moses as a part of the Law. You can find them described in Leviticus 23, as well as in Exodus 12, Exodus 23, Numbers 28, and Deuteronomy 16.

God ordained seven feasts for his people:

- Passover
- Unleavened Bread
- First Fruits
- Harvest (also called Weeks, Shavuot, or Pentecost)
- Trumpets (known today as Rosh Hashanah)
- Atonement (or Yom Kippur)
- Tabernacles (also called Booths or Sukkot)

These were not just holidays like the ones we celebrate—Labor Day or Memorial Day or even Thanksgiving—but were and are God-ordained holy days. The Jewish people were required to observe these festivals annually through special sabbaths and other religious ceremonies. As we'll see, they each have important spiritual significance and prophetic meaning.

How Christ Fulfilled the Feasts

Some of the feasts have agricultural significance; others are remembrances of historical events. But each of them also has a spiritual significance, and they all also have prophetic importance. All seven point to Christ, and in fact Christ has fulfilled—or will fulfill—every one of them. For example, when Paul says in 1 Corinthians 15:20, "But Christ has indeed been raised from the dead, the firstfruits of those who have fallen asleep," he's explicitly referring to the way Jesus has fulfilled the Feast of First Fruits through his resurrection on that very day.

Ultimately, Jesus will fulfill all seven of the feasts. That's why Paul says in Colossians 2:16–17, "Therefore do not let anyone judge you by what you eat or drink, or with regard to a *religious festival* . . . These are a shadow of the things that were to come; *the reality, however, is found in Christ.*" It's also part of what Christ meant when he said in Matthew 5:17, "Do not think that I have come to abolish the Law or the Prophets; I have not come to abolish them *but to fulfill them.*"

The feasts are not just holidays but God-ordained holy days.

The feasts thus constitute a special genre of prophecy, in that each one points to a specific event or accomplishment in the life of the Messiah. Understanding the spiritual meaning of each of the feasts and how each has been (or will be) fulfilled by Christ helps to build our faith. And thinking about how Jesus will complete the feasts that he has not yet fulfilled gives us additional insight into the possible timing of his return.

Let's examine each one.

Passover

The Feast of Passover is a memorial to the Israelites' miraculous delivery out of Egypt. It takes place every year in the spring, on the evening of the fourteenth day of Nisan, the first month of the Hebrew calendar.

On the first Passover, each Israelite family sacrificed a lamb and painted its blood on the door of their house. That night, when the angel of death killed the firstborn of every Egyptian family, he "passed over" the homes marked by the blood of the lambs. The annual celebration of this festival was a reminder of this seminal event in the history of God's people.

Jesus, the Lamb of God, directly fulfilled this feast when he died on the Day of Preparation, Nisan 14. He was crucified at 9:00 a.m. (Mark 15:25), the time when the Jews began preparing for the sacrifice, and died at 3:00 p.m. (Mark 15:33), the very time the lambs were killed. In keeping with the command of Exodus 12:46, none of his bones were broken (John 9:33–36). And, of course, it is his blood, poured out for us, that saves us from the wrath of God, just as the blood of those lambs long ago saved God's people from the angel of death.

Unleavened Bread

The second feast of the Passover season is Unleavened Bread. This festival begins on Nisan 15 (which by Jewish reckoning begins at sunset on Passover, Nisan 14), and lasts for seven days. The first and last days of the festival are special sabbath days.

Unleavened Bread commemorates the deliverance of the Israelites by God out of Egypt, which happened so quickly and unexpectedly they did not have time to bake bread for their journey. Instead, they carried their unleavened dough in kneading troughs as they left (Exod. 12:33–34).

As a result, leaven became a symbol of Israel's old life of slavery in Egypt, and unleavened bread became symbolic of their exodus from that old life—of being delivered and set apart by God. The Feast of Unleavened Bread is thus symbolic of setting aside sin and practicing holiness. As Exodus 13:9 says, "This observance will be like a sign on your hand and a reminder on your forehead that the law of the LORD is to be on your lips."

How did Jesus fulfill the Feast of Unleavened Bread? Luke tells us that on the night before Jesus was crucified, he "took bread, gave thanks and broke it, and gave it to them, saying, 'This is my body given for you; do this in remembrance of me' " (Luke 22:19). The bread Jesus took and broke would have been unleavened bread, symbolizing his perfect, sinless body. By breaking it Jesus demonstrated how that perfect body would be offered as a sacrifice for the sins of the world.

If you've ever seen matzah, the traditional unleavened bread of the Jews, you know that it is pierced and appears to be striped and bruised with scorch marks from the oven, just as the Messiah is described in Isaiah 53:5 (KJV): "But he was wounded for our transgressions, he was bruised for our iniquities; the chastisement for our peace was upon him; and with his stripes we are healed."

Recall that the Last Supper was a Jewish seder, or Passover celebration. The seder ceremony includes fifteen separate steps or stages. During the fourth stage, the *Yachatz*, the leader lifts up the three pieces of matzah, removes the middle piece, and breaks it in half. The smaller half is retained, but the larger piece is then broken again, into five pieces, wrapped in a linen cloth, and hidden (or even buried) until later in the ceremony. Much later, in the twelfth stage, the *Tzafun*, this broken piece of bread, called the *afikomen*, is retrieved and eaten.

All of this is symbolic of the death and burial of Jesus, who, according to John 6:48, is the perfect, unleavened "bread of life." His body was "broken" on Passover, wrapped in linen, and buried on the first day of Unleavened Bread—hidden away in the earth— only to be resurrected from the dead. As John 6:51 says, "Whoever eats this bread will live forever." And as Paul says in 2 Corinthians 5:21, "God made him who had no sin [that is, leaven] to be sin for us, so that in him we might become the righteousness of God."

First Fruits

The third of the Passover feasts is First Fruits. On the day of First Fruits, the Jews were to bring the first sheaves of the barley harvest and wave them before the Lord. The idea was to offer the first fruits of the harvest to God and thus to consecrate the entire coming harvest to him. Spiritually, this feast reminds Jews that it is God who provides the harvest, that everything belongs to God, and that they should put God first.

We've already seen how Jesus fulfilled this festival through his resurrection, by becoming the "firstfruits" of those to be raised from the dead (1 Cor. 15:20–23). Jesus' resurrection from the dead in glory and power represents the "first fruits" of the coming resurrection of God's people. He is the symbolic promise and guarantee of the great kingdom harvest that is to come. And just as the First Fruits offering consecrates the entire harvest, so Christ, the First Fruits of the resurrection, consecrates all of us who belong to him.

Harvest/Pentecost

The Feast of Harvest, or Pentecost as it came to be known by New Testament times, falls fifty days after Nisan 15, the first Sabbath of Unleavened Bread. At first glance it is an agricultural festival, celebrated at the time of the wheat harvest in ancient Israel. Like First Fruits, it required the offering of agricultural sacrifices.

But this holiday also has significant spiritual meaning. By tradition, the Jews believe that it was on this day that Moses received the Torah from God on Mount Sinai. I'm careful to say "by tradition" because there is no biblical connection between Pentecost and the giving of the Law. In Leviticus 23, when Moses ordains the Feast, he doesn't say anything about that date being the date he received the Law—something you'd think he might have mentioned if it were true.

The feasts are a type of prophecy, and each one points to a specific event in the life of the Messiah.

But even if the link between Pentecost and the Law is biblically weak, the significance of this holiday in the history of the church is enormous. It was on the first Pentecost that Jesus sent the Holy Spirit to his disciples (Acts 2). Filled with his power, they immediately began to preach the first gospel sermon, and on that day "about three thousand were added to their number" (Acts 2:41). These three thousand new believers were the "first fruits" of a global harvest of men and women into God's kingdom.

Tabernacles

The Feast of Tabernacles is one of the most joyous Jewish holidays. It celebrates the nation's deliverance from Egypt and the presence of God "tabernacling" with them during the forty-year exodus. It is also a kind of Thanksgiving holiday celebrating God's provision. Leviticus 23:40 instructs the Israelites to "rejoice before the LORD your God for seven days" during this feast.

Leviticus 23:42 requires Jews to erect and live in temporary shelters for the seven days of this feast. For this reason, in Hebrew the feast is called *Sukkot*, from the Hebrew word for "tent" or "booth," *sukkah*. Today, observant Jews still build small shelters in which they eat and sometimes sleep during the feast.

Interestingly, Solomon's temple was dedicated during this feast (1 Kings 8:2). It was during the dedication ceremony that God's Shekinah glory descended to take up residence in the Holy of Holies. Likewise, the Feast of Booths was the first feast celebrated in Jerusalem after Ezra rebuilt the altar following the Babylonian exile (Ezra 3:4).

THE CELEBRATION OF TABERNACLES

In Jesus' day, the observance of Sukkot included a ceremony called the Celebration of the Water-Drawing. On the final day of the feast, a priest would draw water from the Pool of Siloam with a golden pitcher and carry it up the hill to the altar in the temple, where it would be poured out to great rejoicing.

Jesus delivered one of his best-known sermons on this day. According to John 7:37–38,

On the last and greatest day of the festival, Jesus stood and said in a loud voice, "Let anyone who is thirsty come to me and drink. Whoever believes in me, as Scripture has said, rivers of living water will flow from within them."

The ultimate fulfillment of this ceremony will be in the New Jerusalem, when a river of living water will flow from the throne of God (Rev. 22:1).

A related ritual during Sukkot was called the Illumination of the Temple. On the first day of the feast, huge menorahs were lit in the temple courts. The Talmud says that these lamps would give light to "all the courtyards of Jerusalem." This ceremony was symbolic of the presence of God's Shekinah glory with the people.

According to John 8:12, it was in response to this celebration that Jesus revealed that he was the fulfillment of the promise of God's Shekinah glory presence. He said, "I am the light of the world. Whoever follows me will never walk in darkness, but will have the light of life."

And again, this ceremony will be ultimately fulfilled in the New Jerusalem, when according to Revelation 22:5, "There will be no more night. They will not need the light of a lamp or the light of the sun, for the Lord God will give them light."

Was Jesus Born During Tabernacles?

But there is an even more important way in which Christ has fulfilled this feast. It seems likely, from hints Luke provides in his Gospel, that Jesus was born during the Feast of Tabernacles.

In Luke 1, we read that the father of John the Baptist, Zechariah, was a priest "in the order of Abijah," and that he received the promise from Gabriel that his wife, Elizabeth, would bear a son while he was on duty at the temple. We know from 1 Chronicles 24 that the order of Abijah served in the temple in the second half of the fourth month of the Jewish religious calendar, or in June or July on our calendar. Assuming that Zechariah didn't waste any time upon returning home after his service, that means his son, John the Baptist, was likely conceived around July 1.

Table 3: Was Jesus Born at Tabernacles?

Event	Scripture	Month
Gabriel appears to Zechariah	Luke 1:5, 8; 1 Chronicles 24	Late June or early July
John is conceived	Luke 1:23–24	Around July 1
Gabriel visits Mary	Luke 1:26	Around January 1
Birth of John	Luke 1:57–62	Around April 1
Birth of Jesus	Luke 2:1–20	Around October 1

From Luke 1:26, 31 we know that Gabriel appeared to Mary "in the sixth month of Elizabeth's pregnancy" to tell her "you will conceive and give birth to a son." In other words, Jesus was conceived six months after John, probably in the tenth month of the Jewish calendar, or around January 1.

Nine months later would put the birth of Jesus in the seventh month of the Jewish calendar, in late September or perhaps early October, at exactly the time when the fall feasts were being celebrated. So from the best biblical evidence it seems likely that Jesus was born at the time of Tabernacles.

THE ULTIMATE FULFILLMENT

The Feast of Tabernacles ultimately will be fulfilled in Christ's second coming, when he returns to earth permanently, first to establish his thousand-year kingdom and then to rule forever over the new earth. From that point on, he will permanently tabernacle with us. What a great promise that is!

The Remaining Feasts

As we've just seen, during his first coming Jesus fulfilled five of the seven feasts of Israel. But what about the other two feasts, Trumpets and the Day of Atonement? Given how perfectly Jesus has fulfilled the five, it seems certain that he will fulfill the two that remain as well. I believe these two will be fulfilled in the future, when he returns: that the rapture will take place during the Feast of Trumpets and that Jesus' final return will be on the Day of Atonement.

The Feast of Trumpets

The Feast of Trumpets was ordained in Leviticus 23:24–25, which says that it was to be held "on the first day of the seventh month." You may have heard this day called Rosh Hashanah, which means "head of the year." Even though it takes place in the "seventh month" according to Leviticus, over time it has come to be a New Year's Day celebration for the Jewish people.

As commanded, the Jews celebrated this day with loud blasts from the *shofar*, or ram's horn, recognizing the new year and awakening the people to the ten-day period of reflection and repentance leading up to the Day of Atonement. The trumpets would be blown a total of one hundred times on this day: thirty-three sets of three blasts, followed by one long blast, called the final trumpet.

No One Knows the Day or the Hour

There is one important way that Trumpets differs from all the other Feasts: it is the only one that begins on the first day of the month, signified by the new moon. Because Trumpets begins on the first day of a new month (the month of Tishri), in Jesus' day the celebration of this feast could not commence until the new moon had been spotted and the new month officially begun.

> *The phrase "No one knows the day or hour" may be a Jewish idiom describing the Feast of Trumpets.*

The Jews of Jesus' day could count twenty-eight days from one new moon to the next just as well as we can today. But that was not sufficient; the meticulous Jews required that the new moon actually be sighted before the new month could be declared officially. And so they developed a formal system for verifying the new moon, which required the testimony of two reliable witnesses that they had seen it and a formal ruling by the high priest. Once the ruling was issued, the new moon would be announced by the blowing of the shofar, and the celebration would begin.

The Jews also developed a process for communicating the declaration of the new moon to those who did not live in Jerusalem, using messengers and perhaps even signal fires. And because news traveled slowly in those days, the Feast of Trumpets was celebrated over two days (Tishri 1 and 2) so that those who lived far away would not miss it.

In his book *Signs in the Heavens: A Jewish Messianic Perspective of the Last Days & Coming Millennium*, Avi Ben Mordechai says that because of the uncertainty about when the new moon would be seen, until its sighting was officially confirmed, the priests would say that "no one knows the day or the hour" when the feast would begin.[57] In other words, "No one knows the day or the hour" may very well have been a Jewish idiom that described the Feast of Trumpets.

THE RAPTURE AT TRUMPETS?

So when Jesus said, "But about that day or hour no one knows, not even the angels in heaven, nor the Son, but only the Father," he may not have been saying only that no one could know the exact time of his return. He may have been repeating a Jewish expression that described the Feast of Trumpets and thus narrowing down the date of his return to just a couple of days—Tishri 1 and 2—in each year's calendar. Yes, he was saying that no one could know on which of the two days or at what hour he would come. But was he also saying that when he came, it would be in fulfillment of the Feast of Trumpets?

As fellow Jews, Jesus' disciples would have understood immediately what he meant by this idiom. But that meaning has been lost over the centuries, to the extent that his words are now understood to say something almost directly opposite to their original meaning.

Other passages of Scripture also connect the second coming to Trumpets. For example, 1 Corinthians 15:52 says, "*For the trumpet will sound*, the dead will be raised imperishable, and we will be changed." And 1 Thessalonians 4:16–17 promises,

> For the Lord himself will come down from heaven, with a loud command, with the voice of the archangel and *with the trumpet call of God*, and the dead in Christ will rise first. After that, we who are still alive and are left will be caught up together with them in the clouds to meet the Lord in the air.

These verses describe the coming rapture, when the dead in Christ will be raised, those who are alive will be transformed, and we will all go to meet Jesus in the clouds. Paul says this event will be accompanied by "the last trumpet" and "the trumpet call of God"—a reference to the Feast of Trumpets, which will be fulfilled by Christ's initial return at the rapture.

Day of Atonement

The last of the seven annual Feasts is the Day of Atonement, or Yom Kippur. The word *atonement* means "to cover," and this was the day that the sins of the nation were covered by the blood of sacrifice. Yom Kippur is the most solemn of the Jewish Feasts—a day commemorated by fasting and grieving before God.

The Day of Atonement falls ten days after Trumpets, on the tenth of Tishri. The ten days leading up to Yom Kippur, beginning on Rosh Hashanah, are known as the Days of Repentance.

According to Leviticus 16, the Day of Atonement was the one time each year when the high priest could go behind the curtain into the Holy of Holies and be "face to face" with God—but only wearing special garments and only after an elaborate ceremony of washing. The priest would first sacrifice a young bull and sprinkle its blood on the "mercy seat" to atone for his own sin. He would then cast lots to choose between two goats that had been selected for the day. He would sacrifice one of them and sprinkle its blood on the mercy seat to atone for the sins of the people. He would then lay his hands on the other goat—the scapegoat—and confess all the sins of the people, thus symbolically placing the sins of the people on the head of this goat. This goat was then released into the wilderness, symbolizing the removal of the people's sins.

The second coming will fulfill the Day of Atonement.

By tradition, the Jews believed that this was the day that God judged the sins of the entire nation. They believed that the gates of heaven were open during the Days of Repentance that led up to Yom Kippur so that the people's prayers of confession and contrition would be heard. But on this day, the future of every individual would be sealed, those who had observed the day with sincerity would have their names written in the Book of Life, and at the end of the day the Book and the gates of heaven would be closed. So this day was also known as the Day of Judgment—if a person's name was not written in the Book of Life when it was closed, he would not have another opportunity for an entire year. Many Jews still believe these same things today.

Jesus Fulfilled the Day of Atonement

How has Jesus fulfilled the Day of Atonement? First, Christ's death on the cross was the spiritual fulfillment of the Day of Atonement. As Romans 3:25 says, "God presented Christ as a sacrifice of atonement, through the shedding of his blood."

Jesus' fulfillment of the Old Testament sacrificial system and the Day of Atonement is the primary theme of the book of Hebrews. Hebrews 9 describes the sacrificial system and the Day of Atonement and explains how Christ has fulfilled the Old Testament system. It contrasts the Old Testament sacrificial system with Jesus' sacrifice like this:

> The blood of goats and bulls and the ashes of a heifer sprinkled on those who are ceremonially unclean sanctify them so that they are outwardly clean. How much more, then, will the blood of Christ, who through the eternal Spirit offered himself unblemished to God, cleanse our consciences from acts that lead to death, so that we may serve the living God! (Heb. 9:13–14)

What's more, recall that on the Day of Atonement the high priest would go behind the curtain in the temple into the Holy of Holies to be "face to face" with God. Do you remember what happened to that curtain when Christ died? Mark 15:37–38 says, "With a loud cry, Jesus breathed his last. The curtain of the temple was torn in two from top to bottom." By fulfilling the Feast of Yom Kippur, Christ has done away with the need for the curtain and has allowed all who follow him to have a face-to-face relationship with the Father.

THE SECOND COMING

The Jews have long believed that the Messiah would come on the Day of Atonement to save his people once and for all from their sins. Because they misunderstood the prophecies of the Old Testament, they missed his first coming as the Lamb of God who took away the sins of the world—not on the Day of Atonement, but on Passover. But in a sense, they were right, because the Scriptures testify that when he comes back, he will save the remnant of Israel. Zechariah 12:10 says,

> I will pour out on the house of David and the inhabitants of Jerusalem a spirit of grace and supplication. They will look on me, the one they have pierced, and they will mourn for him as one mourns for an only child, and grieve bitterly for him as one grieves for a firstborn son.

This verse speaks of the people having the spirit of grieving and mourning consistent with the observance of Yom Kippur. Romans

11:26–27 promises that on that day, God will "take away their sins" and "all Israel will be saved."

Daniel 9:24 likewise declares,

Seventy "sevens" are decreed for your people and your holy city to finish transgression, to put an end to sin, to atone for wickedness, to bring in everlasting righteousness, to seal up vision and prophecy and to anoint the Most Holy Place.

This prophecy promises that at the end of time, the Jewish people will repent, their sins will be atoned for, everlasting righteousness will be brought in, all prophecies will be fulfilled, and the Most Holy Place will be anointed—all by the return of Christ on a coming Day of Atonement.

Christ in the Feasts

As we've seen in this chapter, Jesus, through his first coming, has fulfilled five of the seven feasts God ordained for Israel:

- He was born on Tabernacles.
- He died on Passover.
- He was buried on Unleavened Bread.
- He rose again on First Fruits.
- He sent the Holy Spirit on Pentecost.

Figure 3: Jesus and the Seven Feasts

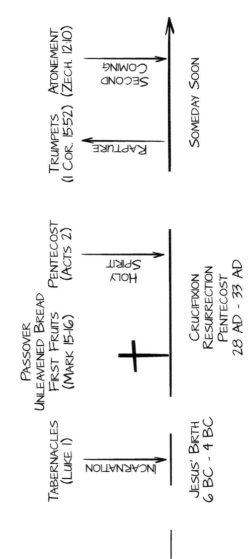

Given that Jesus so perfectly fulfilled those five, is there any doubt that God will work to see the other two fulfilled in him as well? I am convinced

- that the rapture, when Jesus returns to gather his church, will be on the Feast of Trumpets—just as he predicted, on "the hour and day no one knows, but only the Father"—in a year not too far in the future; and
- that his second coming, in glory, to establish his earthly kingdom, will take place on the Day of Atonement, seven years later.

So the next time you hear someone say, "You know, Jesus told us that we can't know when he was coming back," you'll have a story to tell them. And when you tell them that story, you can also let them know that now is the time to prepare for his return—because he's coming back soon.

PART
THREE

Understanding
Our
Hope

11

What Kind of People?

Let's suppose that I'm correct—that Jesus' return is imminent, likely to occur in the next few years. In light of that, what should we be doing? How should we be living? What kind of people ought we to be as this incredible event draws near?

The apostle Peter asks and answers that very question in chapter 3 of his second epistle. He looks ahead to the coming judgment and asks: "Since everything will be destroyed in this way, what kind of people ought you to be?" And he answers like this: "You ought to live holy and godly lives as you look forward to the day of God and speed its coming" (2 Peter 3:11–12). Peter says, first, that we must prepare ourselves for Jesus' return by living holy and godly lives. Second, he says, we should "look forward" to the day of God—that is, Jesus' return—and finally, that we should "speed" the coming of that day. Let's take a look at each part of that command.

Live Holy Lives

When you hear the word *holy*, you probably think of something sacred or exalted. And that's correct. But the Greek word translated "holy," *hagios*, literally means "different, unlike, or other." God is holy because he is transcendent: different from, separate from, and unlike the world and human beings. As he says in his Word, "my thoughts are not your thoughts, neither are your ways my ways" (Isa. 55:8).

The word *holy* also conveys the sense of being set apart, which I think is exactly what Peter has in mind. As we saw in chapter 7, the world will be increasingly godless and wicked as the end draws near—more and more like the days of Noah and Lot. Peter calls for God's people to be different, separate, and set apart from the corroding culture of the last days. As Paul says in Romans 12:2, "Do not conform to the pattern of this world . . ." And as he says in 2 Corinthians 6:17, "'Come out from them and be separate,' says the Lord."

Speaking negatively, this means that we should *not* participate in the world's increasing wickedness. If you want a list, Paul lays out the "deeds of the flesh" in Galatians 5:19–21: "Sexual immorality, impurity and debauchery; idolatry and witchcraft; hatred, discord, jealousy, fits of rage, selfish ambition, dissensions, factions and envy; drunkenness, orgies, and the like." He warns "that those who live like this will not inherit the kingdom of God."

Live Godly Lives

Instead, we should be godly—literally, like God. Thankfully, we have a perfect illustration of what that looks like in Jesus. In John

14:9, when Philip asks Jesus to "show us the Father," Jesus says, "Don't you know me, Philip, even after I have been among you such a long time? Anyone who has seen me has seen the Father."

So if we want to be like God, we should strive to be like Jesus. Again, if you want a list, it's in Galatians 5:22–25:

> The fruit of the Spirit is love, joy, peace, forbearance, kindness, goodness, faithfulness, gentleness and self-control. Against such things there is no law. Those who belong to Christ Jesus have crucified the flesh with its passions and desires. Since we live by the Spirit, let us keep in step with the Spirit.

That last part is crucially important. This list is called the fruit of the Spirit because we can produce it only by the power of the Spirit. So to live a godly life, we need to live by the Spirit.

Looking Forward to That Day

Peter also says we should "look forward to the day of God." In other words, we should live in anticipation and excitement about the return of Christ and the establishment of his kingdom. And if this command was true two thousand years ago, how much truer is it today, when it's possible we'll see God fulfill his promises about his kingdom in our lifetimes?

In the light of passages such as 1 Thessalonians 5:2–6 and Revelation 3:3, one aspect of "looking forward" to that day is to be awake and aware

"Godly" means literally like God, increasingly displaying the fruit of the Spirit.

of the times in which we live. That's exactly why I've written this book: to alert you to the possible soon return of Christ.

But looking forward to that day means more than just being aware that it's near; it also means being eager for his coming. In 2 Timothy 4:8, Paul speaks of a "crown of righteousness" that is in store for him and "all who have *longed for* [Jesus'] appearing." As I've said elsewhere, the return of Christ and the coming of his kingdom is the "blessed hope" for those who love Jesus. That day will be the best day ever—like Christmas, your birthday, and your anniversary, rolled into one, times infinity! As much as we look forward to those days, we should look forward to That Day so much more.

Speeding Its Coming

Peter doesn't just say that we should look forward to that day, but that we should also speed its coming. The Good News Translation says we should "do [our] best to make it come soon" and the ESV says we ought to be "hastening the coming of the day of God." But how can we do that? How is it possible for any of us to do anything to hasten the coming of Jesus?

Recall from chapter 3 that Jesus has given his church a task to complete before he returns: that we are to preach the gospel "in the whole world as a testimony to all nations." He told his disciples that he wouldn't come back until that mission had been accomplished. The one thing that we can do to hasten Jesus' coming is to do our part to finish that task. For all of us, that means praying and actively sharing the good news with our families, friends, and those we encounter in life; for some, it means giving in support of missions, church planters, and Bible translators; and for a few it means becoming missionaries themselves.

If you ask God, he'll show you the role he wants you to play. But all of us should be obedient to Peter's command: we should be "looking forward to" and doing our part to "speed the coming" of that day.

Self-Controlled

The Bible offers other counsel for God's people for living in the last days. In 1 Peter 4:7 (ESV), the apostle tells us, "The end of all things is at hand; therefore be self-controlled and sober-minded . . ."

The Greek word translated "self-controlled" is *sophroneo*, and it literally means sound-minded. Other English versions use "clear-minded," "alert," "sensible," and "serious" to translate this word. "Sober-minded"—or just "sober" in most translations—is the

Self-controlled means that we master our thoughts and emotions.

Greek word *nepho*, which literally means not drunk or not intoxicated. In the New Testament, the word describes having clear judgment, equanimity, temperance, and self-control.

These two words overlap and reinforce one another. The idea is that we should be in control of our thoughts and emotions, not easily distracted by trivial or meaningless things, not carried away by our passions and desires, and not confused but discerning and wise. We want to be able to see what's going on around us and process and respond to it in a rational, even-minded way. This doesn't mean that we're emotionless, like Spock, but instead that we have balance and self-control so that our emotions and desires do not overwhelm and dominate us.

Jesus is coming soon, and we want him to find us grounded, alert, and focused when he does.

Standing Firm

The Bible frequently instructs us to stand firm in our faith. In 1 Corinthians 15:58, Paul says, "Therefore, my dear brothers and sisters, stand firm. Let nothing move you." Four times in four sentences in Ephesians 6 Paul urges us to stand: "against the devil's schemes," "against the day of evil," and "after you've done everything," he says, stand firm. Paul's metaphor is of a soldier resisting a frontal attack, refusing to retreat against an enemy onslaught. He goes on to explain that we do that by being equipped with the "full armor of God": the belt of truth, the breastplate of righteousness, the boots of the gospel, the shield of faith, the helmet of salvation, and the sword of the Spirit. Fully armed with these defenses and weapons, we're prepared to prevail against even the fiercest attack.

In Matthew 24, Jesus warns that things will get tougher for believers and the church in the remaining days before he returns. Persecution will increase, and the wickedness of culture will increasingly infect the church, leading many to fall away from the faith. But, Jesus says, "The one who stands firm to the end will be saved" (Matt. 24:13). While the battle may be fierce, the good news is it won't last much longer, because he is coming soon.

Standing Together

But it's not enough to be equipped—you also need companions in the fight. Rarely does a soldier alone survive an attack, even if he has the best weapons and they are skillfully deployed. The odds of victory increase dramatically when we stand shoulder to shoulder with our fellow believers. When we're fighting together, we can encourage one another. We can guard one another's backs. If one falls, the others can lift him up. If one's armor slips, her companions can help her put it back on.

Things will get tougher for believers and the church in the remaining days before Jesus returns.

This is why being in fellowship with God's people is so important. The Christian life is not meant to be lived in isolation, but in close fellowship with our brothers and sisters. And that's going to be all the more true as we get closer to the Lord's return. This is why Hebrews 10:24–25 urges us to "consider how we may spur one another on toward love and good deeds, not giving up meeting together, as some are in the habit of doing, but encouraging one another—*and all the more as you see the Day approaching.*"

COVID-19 dramatically affected church attendance in 2020. For weeks, virtually every church in the United States was closed, but even as some churches regathered, many chose not to attend in person. More will likely come back as the fear of the virus fades, but experts predict that a significant percentage of those who were attending church pre-COVID may never return to physical gatherings. Of course, those changes come on top of the existing accelerating trends away from church attendance, especially among younger people, that we considered in chapter 8.

The Bible compares the church to a body and a building, where each part or each brick is a vital component of the whole. Each believer has been gifted with special abilities or aptitudes that he or she is intended to use for the benefit of others and the whole. Exercising those gifts requires us to be together.

What's more, much of the fruit of the Spirit is revealed only in relationship with others. Think of love, patience, and kindness, for example: they cannot be practiced and perfected except in close relationship with others. Likewise, consider the numerous "one another" commands in the New Testament: bear with one another, forgive one another, serve one another, love one another, and so on. Again, exercising those "one another" muscles requires us to be in connection with other people.

I've always wondered about the tag the writer of Hebrews adds to this exhortation: "and all the more as you see the Day approaching." For a long time, I assumed that this was included to suggest that there was no time limit on this requirement—that it would continue to apply through the church age. But now, as I see the Day approaching and I see many separating from the church, I wonder if the Spirit, in his amazing wisdom, didn't include this phrase as a specific instruction to us. Was he warning us that in the last days, as we experience the increasing persecution that will be part of the buildup to the tribulation, we would need to be joined with one another through the church more than ever?

So, if you're already connected to a church, stay connected. If possible, get even more tightly connected. If you don't have a church, let me encourage you to find one that you will join, attend, and serve. If not a church, then find a group of believing friends who will meet regularly to worship God and practice your "one anothers." And do this all the more as you see the Day approaching.

Generous

If you were certain Jesus was coming back soon, how would it affect your giving? Most of us are saving and investing for retirement, but what if we were convinced that retirement was never to come? Would we give more?

In Luke 12:15–21, Jesus told a sobering parable about the reality that his return—or our departure to be with him—is imminent, and that on that day our material possessions will no longer be of any value to us. In that story he speaks of a certain man whose ground "yielded an abundant harvest." Not knowing what to do with the excess, he said, "This is what I'll do. I will tear down my barns and build bigger ones, and there I will store my surplus grain. And I'll say to myself, 'You have plenty of grain laid up for many years. Take life easy; eat, drink and be merry.'" But God says to the man, "You fool! This very night your life will be demanded from you. Then who will get what you have prepared for yourself?" Jesus concludes, "This is how it will be with whoever stores up things for themselves but is not rich toward God."

Our culture is exceedingly materialistic, and it is so easy for believers to get caught up in the world's thinking that more is always better. As a result, we end up stockpiling more than we need or can ever use, instead of giving generously to God's kingdom work and the needs of others. We fall into the trap that Jesus warned about: thinking that life "consists of an abundance of possessions."

You may not think this parable applies to you because you're not rich. But as an American of even modest means, you're almost certainly in the top few percent of the wealthy on the planet. And all of us—rich, poor, and in the middle—face the temptation of basing our significance and security on material things instead of trusting in God to meet our needs and give purpose to our lives. So Jesus' warning about "bigger barns" is really for all of us.

It is easy for believers to get caught up in the world's thinking that more is always better.

There is nothing wrong with planning for the future and preparing for retirement. The Old Testament specifically commends those who leave an inheritance to their children. But I've been thinking recently about how shameful it would be to have Jesus come back and find me standing beside new barns I'd built to store all kinds of stuff I would never use.

As we see the Day approaching, let's step out in faith, giving sacrificially—literally, as if there were no tomorrow. Let's not fall into the trap of building bigger barns, hoarding up for ourselves what we can't use and don't need.[58]

Working

At the conclusion of Jesus' Olivet Discourse in Matthew 24, we find a series of parables that show us how we should live as we await Jesus' return. In the first of these, the Parable of the Wise Servant,

Jesus exhorts his people to be hard at work, in service to him and to the church, right up until the end. He says,

> "Who then is the faithful and wise servant, whom the master has put in charge of the servants in his household to give them their food at the proper time? It will be good for that servant whose master finds him doing so when he returns. Truly I tell you, he will put him in charge of all his possessions. (vv. 45–47)

There are different ideas about what Jesus has in mind when he says, "Give them their food at the proper time." My opinion is that this phrase describes meeting the needs of God's people, and that "the faithful and wise servant" is any one of God's people—not just church leaders and pastors—who uses his or her gifts to meet those needs. As Peter says in 1 Peter 4:10, "Each of you should use whatever gift you have received to serve others, as faithful stewards of God's grace in its various forms." Paul makes the same point in Romans 12, where he urges us to use our gifts diligently for the benefit of our brothers and sisters—to prophesy, serve, teach, encourage, give, lead, and show mercy in accordance with the gifts we've received.

And notice the promise of reward: Jesus says that he will put those who are found working when he returns "in charge of all his possessions." That's the same idea found in the Parable of the Talents: that those who are faithful in "investing" the gifts we've been given by God will be entrusted with greater responsibilities: "Well done, good and faithful servant. You have been faithful over a little; I will set you over much" (Matt. 25:21, ESV).

In this same parable, Jesus contrasts the wise servant with another he calls "wicked." This servant represents a believer who squanders his gifts and his opportunity, abusing his "fellow servants" and living a worldly lifestyle, because he begins to think his master will never return. Jesus says that when he comes, he will deal severely with such a servant, promising to "cut him to pieces and assign him a place with the hypocrites" (Matt. 24:48–51).

Most of us are somewhere between these two extremes: we're not dissolute like the wicked servant, but we also aren't pursuing the "good works, which God has prepared in advance for us to do" (Eph. 2:10) as eagerly as we might. Subconsciously, we believe that we'll have time later to get more involved in the church and God's kingdom work. We're working hard in our jobs and raising our kids and don't feel we have the time and energy to devote to God's work. We're also easily sidetracked by the glut of distractions that surround us.

But if Jesus is coming soon, now is the time to heed his warning and seize the opportunities he has given us. Are you using your gifts to the best of your ability for the good of God's people? If not, make today the day you reset your priorities and put your work for God's kingdom at the top of your list. He's coming soon, and he wants to find you at work.

Prepared

Next, Jesus tells the Parable of the Ten Virgins (Matt. 25:1–13). In this story, the bridegroom represents Jesus, and the coming of the bridegroom symbolizes his return. The banquet represents the celebration of the reunion of Jesus with his people. The virgins are ten people who have been invited to the wedding banquet. They represent the church in the days of the Lord's return. Jesus says that five of the virgins were prepared, with plenty of oil for their lamps; they are welcomed into the wedding banquet. The others were not prepared, and they were not allowed in.

What does the oil represent? From the story, we know that oil must be something necessary for admission to the banquet—in other words, it symbolizes something that the virgins must have in hand *before* the bridegroom returns. It's clear that what is needed is not something that can be borrowed from another person—we have to acquire it for ourselves as our own possession. When the foolish virgins ask the wise, "Give us some of your oil," they reply,

Sadly, Jesus indicates that many will be unprepared for his return.

"No, there may not be enough for both us and you. Instead, go to those who sell oil and buy some for yourselves" (v. 9)

In the context, then, the oil must represent genuine faith, or perhaps for the presence of the Holy Spirit as evidence of genuine faith. Is there anything else that would by its absence disqualify someone from entering the wedding feast? The Bible teaches that we are saved by grace through faith in Jesus Christ, so no one who has saving faith will be excluded from the banquet, but no one who lacks it will be admitted.

Authentic Faith

If that's right, the five wise virgins are true believers, while the five foolish virgins represent people who would claim to be believers who don't have genuine saving faith. They're the same folks Jesus speaks about in Matthew 7:21–23 when he says,

> "Not everyone who says to me, 'Lord, Lord,' will enter the kingdom of heaven, but only the one who does the will of my Father who is in heaven. Many will say to me on that day, 'Lord, Lord, did we not prophesy in your name and in your name drive out demons and in your name perform many miracles?' Then I will tell them plainly, 'I never knew you. Away from me, you evildoers!' "

This is a serious and sobering teaching, warning that at Jesus' return there will be people who look like Christians, who hang out with Christians, and who would say they are Christians, but who are not saved. Jesus is saying that anything less than authentic, Spirit-filled faith cannot save us.

A person must be truly born again to enter God's kingdom—as Jesus told Nicodemus, "No one can see the kingdom of God unless they are born again" and "no one can enter the kingdom of God unless they are born of water and the Spirit" (John 3:3, 5). It isn't enough to go to church, pray, give, go on mission trips, or, as Jesus says, to prophesy or even to drive out demons in his name. We have to be in relationship with him—he has to live in us through the presence of the Holy Spirit.

Sadly, Jesus indicates that many will be unprepared for his return. According to Matthew 7:23, Jesus will tell "many" on that day, "I never knew you." And while we should not read too much into the details of parables, it's worth noting that Jesus says that half of the virgins in the story were unprepared.

Continuing

So how can we know that we're prepared? First John 2:28 says, "And now, dear children, continue in him, so that when he appears we may be confident and unashamed before him at his coming." The word *continue* in this verse is the same Greek word—*meno*—translated "remain" or "abide" in John 15:5, when Jesus tells his disciples, "I am the vine; you are the branches. If you remain in me and I in you, you will bear much fruit; apart from me you can do nothing."

> *All of our power for living the Christian life comes from and through our connection with Jesus.*

The idea is that all of our power for living the Christian life comes from and through our connection with Jesus. If we remain in him and he in us, we'll have power for everything we've talked about in this chapter: for holy and godly living, for being self-controlled, for standing firm, for generosity, and for our work for him. Apart from him, though, none of this will be possible.

First John 2 reiterates this idea in the context of the return of Christ. John's message is that by continuing in Jesus we can approach his return with confidence, knowing that our lamps are filled with oil. If we continue in him, John says, we will be unashamed when we see him face to face.

What does it look like to remain, abide, and continue in Christ? That's a profound question, but if you're

- striving to obey his commands,
- pursuing a life of repentance,

- increasingly seeking his guidance,
- investing in your relationship with him and his people,
- seeking to be more and more like him, and
- demonstrating increasing fruit of the Spirit,

that's solid evidence that you possess the oil you'll need on that day to be welcomed into the banquet.

Examine Yourself

In 2 Corinthians 13:5, Paul warns the Corinthians, "Examine yourselves to see whether you are in the faith; test yourselves." As I have been writing this section, I have been doing just that, thinking about my life and whether there is anything counterfeit or superficial about my relationship with Jesus. (And, yes, a couple of things came to mind.) I think that very act—the willingness to ask the question and then act on the honest answer—is evidence of the kind of saving faith Jesus is calling for us to have. I urge you to engage in that exercise and then, by the power of the Holy Spirit, to begin to add to your life whatever needs to be added or to remove whatever needs to be taken away.

Like a Bride

In Ephesians 5:25–27, Paul reminds us that we—the church—are the bride of Christ:

> Christ loved the church and gave himself up for her to make her holy, cleansing her by the washing with water through the word, and to present her to himself as a radiant church, without stain or wrinkle or any other blemish, but holy and blameless.

As we prepare for the coming our bridegroom, let's commit to living out the truth of the promise that we are a bride "without stain or wrinkle or any other blemish, but holy and blameless." Let's strive to live holy and godly lives so that when he comes, he will find us ready, with plenty of oil in our lamps. Let's exercise the gifts God has given us, doing the good works he has prepared in advance for us to do, and taking hold of the rewards he has promised. Let's practice self-control and let's stand firm against the increasing corruption of our culture and the personal attacks of the enemy. Let's get as closely connected as we can, practicing all the "one anothers" together—and all the more as we see the day approaching. Let's "continue in him so that when he appears, we may be confident and unashamed before him at his coming."

And let's not wait to get started. Because he is coming soon.

THE GOSPEL COMES TO

The Wadimar

The Hindu Wadimar people are businesspeople—among the most successful in the world. They are high-caste, wealthy, and powerful, but they are spiritually lost. There is no record of even one Wadimar being a follower of Jesus.

One day recently, a young woman named Anuja approached an influential Wadimar couple. Because Anuja is herself high caste, they politely invited her into their home for tea.

Anuja is a Jesus follower who is investing her life to take the gospel to the unengaged people groups in her country—groups like the Wadimar where there have never been any believers.

As Anuja enjoyed tea with the couple, she learned that the man was suffering from severe back and neck pain. Doctors had tried everything but could not help. Anuja offered to pray for him in Jesus' name, and he readily accepted. She prayed, and God instantly healed him!

Over the next few days, two other Wadimar women were also healed in the name of Jesus—one of metastatic breast cancer and one of a throat tumor. Word of these miraculous healings spread rapidly, and before long thirteen Wadimar had prayed to receive Christ. They became the first Wadimar believers—ever!

A house church has now been planted in their city. By God's grace, this small group will be the beginning of a powerful movement of the gospel among the Wadimar people.

The gospel has come to the Wadimar.

12

No Eye Has Seen

In this book we've explored ten biblical clues about the timing of Jesus' return. Considered together, the clues strongly suggest that Jesus will be coming back soon. While I haven't tried to pin it down to a day or even to a year, my conclusion is that he is likely to come back in the next few years—within the lifetime of most people reading this book. As I said in the introduction, some generation will be privileged to witness his return. Could it be ours? I think it's likely.

But the return of Christ is not the end for God's people—it's a new beginning! His return will bring the present age to an end but will usher in an eternity living with and serving Jesus and the Father on a new Earth created specifically for us. So let's wrap up with a look ahead—a consideration of what Jesus' return will bring about for those who love him.

The Rapture

I believe the first event in the return of Christ will be the rapture, when God's people from around the world are gathered to him. The primary teaching about the rapture is found in 1 Thessalonians 4:16–18, which says,

> For the Lord himself will come down from heaven, with a loud command, with the voice of the archangel and with the trumpet call of God, and the dead in Christ will rise first. After that, we who are still alive and are left will be caught up together with them in the clouds to meet the Lord in the air. And so we will be with the Lord forever. Therefore encourage one another with these words.

The Greek word translated "caught up" is *harpazo*, which means to seize, catch up, snatch away, or carry off. The idea is that Jesus will return to the earth without actually setting foot on it; that he will issue "a loud command"; that the dead in Christ will be resurrected; that all of them, along with all believers who are alive at that time, will be "gathered to him" in the air; and that he will take us from there to heaven.

There is disagreement about the timing of the rapture, but I believe it will take place before the beginning of the tribulation. I base this opinion on Paul's assurances in 1 Thessalonians 1:10 that Jesus "rescues us from the coming wrath," and 1 Thessalonians 5:9, which promises, "For God did not appoint us to suffer wrath." During the tribulation, God's wrath will be poured out on the world in judgment for sin, but I believe the church will not be present for that judgment because "we have not been appointed to suffer wrath."

However, it is important to remember that the church will experience increasing persecution as the day of the Lord approaches—some of which might be so severe that we think we're living in the tribulation, as the Thessalonians themselves apparently thought. Even if we are delivered from the tribulation, the last few years before Jesus comes for his church will not be easy.

Transformed

Just before we are raptured, Paul teaches in 1 Corinthians 15:51–52, we will be transformed:

> Listen, I tell you a mystery: We will not all sleep, *but we will all be changed*—in a flash, in the twinkling of an eye, at the last trumpet. For the trumpet will sound, the dead will be raised imperishable, and we will be changed.

When that last trumpet blows, the dead in Christ will be raised in new, "imperishable" bodies, and the bodies of those who are alive will be instantly transformed.

The Bible promises that all believers will receive new glorified resurrection bodies.

What will these new bodies be like? Paul gives us a hint in Philippians 3:21, when he says that on that day Jesus "will transform our lowly bodies *so that they will be like his glorious body.*" Likewise, in 1 Corinthians 15:42–44 he says,

> The body that is sown is perishable, it is raised imperishable; it is sown in dishonor, it is raised in glory; it is sown

in weakness, it is raised in power; it is sown a natural body, it is raised a spiritual body.

It's difficult to know exactly what these descriptions mean. What is a "spiritual body" after all? But from what we can understand, we know that these new bodies are going to be amazing.

Imperishable

For one thing, our new bodies will be "imperishable," no longer subject to death and decay. If you're under thirty, that might not mean much to you, but those of us who are over sixty are looking forward to the end of all the aches, pains, weaknesses, and illnesses that are part of having a "perishable," aging body. We will literally enjoy those new bodies forever, and they will never break down and never grow old.

Glorious

For another thing, our new bodies will be raised in glory. I think this might be Paul's poetic way of saying that our new eternal bodies will no longer have what the Bible calls a "sin nature" or "flesh"—*sarx* in the Greek. This "flesh" is characterized by ungodly "passions and desires" (Gal. 5:24) that are "constantly fighting" with the desires of the Spirit, "so you are not free to carry out your good intentions" (Gal. 5:17 NLT). As Paul explains in Romans 7, the Christian life is a continual life-and-death struggle between the flesh and our new, godly nature.

The Bible teaches that our old nature is inherited from our ancestor Adam and is somehow endemic to our physical bodies. That's what Paul means when he says in Romans 7:24, "What a wretched man I am! Who will rescue me from this body of death?" He's saying that we won't be free of "the flesh" and its brokenness until we're free of our mortal bodies.

But here's the good news: the new bodies we will receive at the rapture will no longer have a sin nature. The internal struggle that Paul describes in Romans 7 will be over. From that point on, we'll do only "the good we want to do" without any opposition from that old nature, which will have been done away with once and for all.

That sounds pretty awesome to me. After years of pitched battle and slow progress toward personal holiness (including, sadly, many setbacks), it will be unbelievable finally to be free of that old man. I won't miss him.

Powerful

Paul says that our new bodies will have "power." I wonder if by "power" he means that our new bodies will have supernatural abilities, like Jesus' resurrection body. Jesus' resurrection body was clearly physical—he ate food and Thomas and Mary touched him—but it also had supernatural power and abilities. For example, he could enter locked rooms, appearing and departing suddenly. Could it be that our new bodies will allow us to teleport from place to place? Might we have increased mental capabilities, like telepathy? There's no way to know for sure, but the fact remains: compared to our current "weak" bodies, our new bodies will be bodies of "power."

Real Bodies

One final point here—something I don't want anyone to miss. In the common view of heaven—I call it "Bugs Bunny Heaven" because it's depicted this way in the cartoons—we exist eternally as spirits without physical bodies, floating among the clouds, with halos, playing harps. There is literally nothing correct about that image.

First, the Bible makes clear that we will have real, physical bodies for eternity. We will not exist as spirits only—our bodies will be raised. We'll have faces and names. We'll eat and drink, worship, work, and (probably) play in our glorified bodies.

Paul emphasizes the importance of the resurrection in 1 Corinthians 15:16–17, when he says, "For if the dead are not raised, then Christ has not been raised either. And if Christ has not been raised, your faith is futile . . ." Paul wanted no part of an eternal life without a body, and neither do I. Thankfully, as he says a few verses later, "But Christ has indeed been raised from the dead, the firstfruits of those who have fallen asleep" (v. 20).

> *One of the great blessings of eternity will be our reunion with believing loved ones who have preceded us in death.*

What's more, we will not float among the clouds for very long but will return to and dwell on the earth—a New Earth—forever. And we won't just waste away each day plucking on harps; we'll have work to do for God forever and ever.

Reunion

One of the great blessings of eternity will be our reunion with believing loved ones who have preceded us in death. They will be raised, and their bodies will be transformed along with ours. We'll experience joyful reunions with family members and friends from whom we have been separated—reunions that will include smiles, hugs, and kisses, thanks to our new bodies—and we'll enjoy intimate relationships with them for eternity.

We'll also experience "reunion" with people we've never met in this life but with whom we share important connections. For example, if you've supported missionary work, you have a connection with the people who were brought to Christ through that effort. Even though you've never met those people and couldn't communicate with them today if you did, you'll have the joy of meeting them, exploring your kingdom connection, and praising Jesus together for his goodness in both of your lives. I can't wait to meet some of my new friends.

Unified

In chapter 3, I explained that God's purpose for the world's twelve thousand nations is to bring them all together in the body of Christ. In Ephesians 2:14–16, Paul says,

> For he himself is our peace, who has made the two groups one and has destroyed the barrier, the dividing wall of hostility . . . His purpose was to create in himself one new humanity out of the two, thus making peace, and in one body to reconcile both of them to God through the cross, by which he put to death their hostility.

While we should be seeing this kind of unity in our churches today—men and women of every race and ethnicity coming together under the banner of the gospel—the goal of complete unity will not be accomplished until Jesus returns for us. But on that day—the day he comes back for his bride, the church—all racism and ethnic division will be done away with once and for all. I think we will retain our identities and cultural differences, but those differences will no longer be the source of fear and hatred. We will be truly unified as one people through the blood of Jesus Christ. It will be an amazing day.

The Wedding Supper

In Jesus' day, marriage began with a contract between the parents of the bride and the bridegroom and the payment of a bride price, either by the groom or his father, followed by a period of betrothal that would last as long as a year. At that time, the groom and his friends would come to the house of the bride in the evening. She and her friends would then join them for a torchlit parade through the streets to his father's house, where the marriage would be consummated. Finally, the bride and groom would join with their friends for a great feast that might continue for up to seven days.

One of the metaphors the Bible uses to describe the church is "the bride of Christ," and there are interesting parallels between our relationship with Jesus and the wedding customs of his day. For instance, the marriage contract is symbolic of the new covenant between God and his people through the blood of Christ, which is symbolic of the bride price. The betrothal represents the period in which we're now living: the bridegroom has returned to his Father's house to prepare a place for us, and we are awaiting his return. That torchlit parade symbolizes the rapture, when the bridegroom, Christ, comes to claim his bride and take us to his Father's house in heaven.

And that leaves the wedding supper of the Lamb, which will follow the rapture. We read about this feast in Revelation 19:9: "Blessed are those who are invited to the wedding supper of the Lamb!" The wedding supper will be a joyous celebration of the beginning of a new, eternal, intimate phase of our union with Jesus. Amazingly, Luke 12:37 says that Jesus himself will "dress himself to serve" and will "come and wait on" us as we "recline at the table."

In chapter 3 we saw that the bride will include men and women from every one of the world's twelve thousand people groups. If you've traveled much, you know that people in different places enjoy a wide variety of foods, some of which are quite different from what I'm used to. I love steak and potatoes, but my dear Nigerian friend Daniel likes nothing better than his pounded yam and egusi soup. Can you imagine the diversity of the delicacies at the Wedding Feast, where our bridegroom, Jesus Christ, who desires to please his bride, offers each of us whatever food we prefer? It will be amazing.

In Jesus' day, wedding feasts could last for up to seven days. Is it possible that the wedding supper of the Lamb might last for the entire seven *years* between the rapture and Christ's final return? We can't be sure, but it would not surprise me if it does. What a party it will be!

Rewards

The familiar verses Ephesians 2:8–9 affirm that works have *nothing* to do with our salvation—we are saved by grace, through faith, not by anything we do. But the very next verse, verse 10, explains that work has *everything* to do with our lives as believers: that "we are

God's handiwork, created in Christ Jesus to do good works, which God prepared in advance for us to do."

The Bible teaches that God has not only saved us to do good works and prepared those works for us to do but has also equipped us for them by giving us spiritual gifts. And if all of that wasn't enough, God has also promised to reward us for work we do in his name.

In the Scriptures God repeatedly promises to reward our good works. For example, Matthew 16:27 says, "For the Son of Man is going to come in his Father's glory with his angels, and then *he will reward each person* according to what they have done." Hebrews 6:10 says, "God is not unjust; he will not forget your work and the love you have shown him as you have helped his people and continue to help them." Revelation 22:12 promises, "Look, I am coming soon! *My reward is with me, and I will give to each person according to what they have done.*"

Our works will be judged and our rewards received sometime during the seven-year period between the rapture and the final return of Christ, at what is called the bema judgment. Paul writes about this in Romans 14 and in 2 Corinthians 5:10: "For we must all appear before the judgment seat [bema] of Christ, so that each of us may receive what is due us for the things done while in the body, whether good or bad."

At the bema, everything we've done as believers will be reviewed and evaluated. As Paul says in 1 Corinthians 3, all our works for Jesus will be tested with fire. Some things—good works Paul compares to "gold, silver, and precious stones"—will survive the test and will result in rewards. Other things—works of "wood, hay, and straw"—will burn up. In context, those things seem to represent not evil deeds but "good works" done poorly—perhaps out of selfish ambition or fear or compulsion and not out of faith and love. There will be no rewards for these acts.

As Paul makes clear, this judgment has nothing to do with our salvation. Even if everything we bring burns at the *bema*, we "will be saved." We'll enter eternity without rewards, but we will nevertheless enjoy eternity with Jesus and with God. Our salvation does not depend on the quality of our works: we are not saved by anything we do, but by faith in Jesus Christ.

It's important to remember that our judge at the bema will be our brother, friend, and Savior Jesus Christ, who loves us and gave himself for us. He is for us and his desire is to commend us. While his judgment will be perfect and just, I am confident that he will also judge us graciously and lovingly and that we will receive more than we think we deserve.

It's hard to say exactly what form these promised rewards will take. The Scriptures speak of crowns (1 Corinthians 9), garments (Revelation 19), and treasure in heaven (1 Timothy 6). From the Parable of the Ten Minas in Luke 19, it seems that one form of reward will be increased authority and responsibility in the millennial kingdom and perhaps even into eternity: " 'Well done, my good servant!' his master replied. 'Because you have been trustworthy in a very small matter, take charge of ten cities' " (Luke 19:17).

In the Scriptures God repeatedly promises to reward the good works of his people.

The idea seems to be that our faithfulness in our work for Jesus in this life qualifies us for higher degrees of responsibility in his kingdom. Jesus suggests this when he says, in Luke 16:10–11, "Whoever can be trusted with very little can also be trusted with much, and whoever is dishonest with very little will also be dishonest with much. So if you have not been trustworthy in handling worldly wealth, who will trust you with true riches?"

I hope the idea of eternal rewards fills you with joyful anticipation. But if you're wondering whether you've accomplished anything for Jesus that will survive the test of the bema, now is the time to get to work. What has the Spirit gifted you to do? What opportunities has God put in your path? Now is the time to begin exercising those gifts and seizing those opportunities. You'll enjoy the fruits of that labor for a long time to come.[59]

Armageddon

While we are with Jesus in heaven, celebrating our marriage to him and receiving our rewards, God will be pouring out judgment on the earth. At the end of that seven-year tribulation, we will return with Jesus to the earth. Zechariah 14 tells us that on that day all the nations of the world, under the leadership of the antichrist, will be gathered against Jerusalem. But "then the LORD will go out and fight against those nations, as he fights on a day of battle" (v. 3).

This battle is commonly called Armageddon, and you can find it described in Revelation 19:11–21. Those verses describe the forces arrayed at the battle: on one side Jesus Christ and "the armies of heaven . . . riding on white horses and dressed in fine linen, white and clean"; on the other, "the beast and the kings of the earth and their armies." "The armies of heaven" describes the church and, perhaps, angels who will fight alongside us. This battle will be a rout—the world's army will be destroyed, and its leaders, the beast (that's the antichrist), and his false prophet will be captured and cast into the "fiery lake of burning sulfur" forever.

The Millennium

Following his victory at Armageddon, Jesus will take up the throne of his ancestor David and will begin to rule over the entire earth from Jerusalem. Zechariah 14:9 promises, "The LORD will be king over the whole earth. On that day there will be one LORD, and his name the only name."

According to Revelation 20:6, this period of Christ's rule on this earth shall last for one thousand years. We—the church—"will be priests of God and of Christ and will reign with him for a thousand years."

The Bible has a lot to say about this thousand-year reign of Christ, commonly called the millennium. During this period, the earth will be populated by those who survived the tribulation and by their descendants, who will enjoy supernaturally long life spans. According to Isaiah 65:20, "the one who dies at a hundred will be thought a mere child; the one who fails to reach a hundred will be considered accursed."

According to Revelation 20:3, Satan will be bound in "the Abyss" and will be constrained from "deceiving the nations anymore until the thousand years were ended." While the mortal people of that day will still have a sin nature and will still sin, Satan's absence will make it much easier for them to resist their fleshly desires and live righteously.

The millennium will be a time of unprecedented peace, justice, righteousness, and prosperity on the earth. Describing Jesus' reign, Isaiah 2:4 says that the nations will "beat their swords into plowshares and their spears into pruning hooks" and that "nation will not take up sword against nation, nor will they train for war anymore," describing a time of perfect peace and security. This peace is so universal that, according to Isaiah 11:6 (NASB), it extends to the animals as well: "And the wolf will dwell with the lamb, and the leopard will lie down with the young goat . . ."

The millennium will be a time of unmatched prosperity. The prophet Amos describes it poetically by saying that "the days are coming . . . when the reaper will be overtaken by the plowman and the planter by the one treading grapes" (Amos 9:13).

It also will be a time of worldwide righteousness and godliness. Habakkuk 2:14 says, "For the earth will be filled with the knowledge of the glory of the LORD as the waters cover the sea."

The Final Rebellion

At the end of the millennium, Satan "will be released from his prison and will go out to deceive the nations" (Rev. 20:7–8), stirring them up into rebellion against Jesus and his kingdom. It's hard to imagine how people will be so quickly led into rebellion after experiencing one thousand years of Jesus' perfect rule, but the Bible says it will happen. I think this will be God's way of proving once and for all that it is only by his grace that anyone submits to him; left to their own devices, people will always rebel.

But this rebellion will be quickly overcome. Revelation 20:9–10 promises that "fire came down from heaven and devoured" the enemies of God, and that "the devil, who deceived them, was thrown into the lake of burning sulfur," where he, the beast, and the false prophet "will be tormented day and night for ever and ever."

At last, after that final rebellion, our enemy, Satan, will be done away with once and for all.

The Great White Throne

According to Revelation 20, following this final battle, every person who has ever lived will be raised to life and will give an account of themselves to God at his great white throne. Keep in mind that the dead in Christ will have been raised at the rapture and that the martyrs of the great tribulation will have been raised after the Battle of Armageddon. Therefore, those who are raised in this second resurrection will be those who died apart from Christ. They will be judged individually "according to what they had done," and "anyone whose name was not found written in the book of life was thrown into the lake of fire" (Rev. 20:13, 15).

The New Heaven and Earth

Finally, after all of that, God promises that he will recreate the universe. Revelation 21:1 says, "Then I saw 'a new heaven and a new earth,' for the first heaven and the first earth had passed away . . ." We can only guess what this new creation will be like. Will the same laws of physics apply? Will there be new kinds of plants and animals? Will the new heavens have stars, planets, and galaxies?

God will also create a beautiful city—the New Jerusalem—where we will live with him forever. According to the description in Revelation 21, this new city will be immense and spectacular, built of and decorated with every kind of precious stone. I think it's this New Jerusalem that Jesus was talking about when he told his disciples he was going "to prepare a place for" them (John 14:2). Jesus, the Divine Carpenter, has been working for nearly two thousand years to build this new city, which will be our home for eternity. It's going to be something.

God promises that at the end of this age he will recreate the universe.

Listen to John's description of what life will be like in this new creation:

> And I heard a loud voice from the throne saying, "Look! God's dwelling place is now among the people, and he will dwell with them. They will be his people, and God himself will be with them and be their God. 'He will wipe every tear from their eyes. There will be no more death' or mourning or crying or pain, for the old order of things has passed away." He who was seated on the throne said, "I am making everything new!" (Rev. 21:3–5)

Did you catch all of that? John says:

God will live with us. In the beginning, God walked with Adam in the Garden. In the end, he will live with us in the city. When it's all said and done, we don't go to live with him in heaven; he comes to live with us on the new earth. We'll see him face to face and enjoy his personal presence forever. We'll be "his people" and he will be "our God"—a degree of intimacy and familiarity we cannot conceive today.

He will wipe away every tear. All of us will experience sadness during the last days. We'll regret sins we committed or opportunities and rewards we missed. We'll mourn loved ones who are not with us for eternity. But God promises to comfort us personally, wiping away every tear. And from that point on, there will be no more crying or pain—only the joy of being in continual relationship with our Maker and Redeemer.

Death will be a memory. We'll never again experience death or its predecessor, decay. There won't even be pain! According to Revelation 20, death itself will be destroyed at the great white throne judgment and will be "thrown into the lake of fire." At last, our enemy, death, will be done away with once and for all.

Everything will be new! When the story of this creation has come to an end, God will create an entirely new reality for his people. We will enjoy exploring and learning about this new creation forever and ever.

John goes on to tell us that the New Jerusalem—our eternal home—will not have a temple because "the Lord God Almighty and the Lamb are its temple" (Rev. 21:22). In other words, God and Jesus will live openly in the city, not confined to any sacred building. The city will not need the sun or the moon to shine on it for light, because "the glory of God gives it light, and the Lamb is its lamp" (v. 23). Its gates will never "be shut," signaling that it will exist forever in perfect peace and safety (v. 25). There will be a "river of the water of life, as clear as crystal, flowing from the throne of God and of the Lamb down the middle of the great street of the city," and along the river will be "the tree of life" (vv. 1, 2). The New Jerusalem will be a place of abundant, overflowing life.

Revelation 22 also teaches that we will serve God forever. In other words, we'll work. But it promises that "no longer will there be any curse" (v. 3), so our work will be different from anything we've ever experienced. Instead of endless toil just to stay ahead of the decay, our work will be fruitful and the things we create will endure permanently. Part of our work will be to "reign for ever and ever" (v. 5). It's not clear over whom we will reign, but God's promise is that we will rule with him and his Son forever over the new creation he has made for us.

No Eye Has Seen

All of that is amazing, but I don't think it begins to capture how incredible our eternal existence will be. In fact, I don't believe that it is possible to describe it. In 1 Corinthians 2:9 (NLT), Paul teases us by saying,

"No eye has seen, no ear has heard,
and no mind has imagined
what God has prepared
for those who love him."

Any attempt to describe eternity must fall short, because if it can be written down, it can be imagined. Even the words John uses to describe the things he saw are undoubtedly an inadequate description of what he actually witnessed.

I can imagine quite a lot: being able to fly, traveling to distant galaxies, speaking hundreds of languages, having multiple mental conversations simultaneously, and many other astounding things. But God has promised that what he has in store for us exceeds by far even the expanse of our imaginations. It is going to be unimaginably awesome.

He's Coming Soon

And we don't have long to wait. I've made the case in this book that Jesus is coming soon—perhaps in the next year or two, perhaps a little later, but surely very soon. The Great Commission is nearing completion. Israel has been regathered now for nearly a generation. An abomination has been crouching on the Temple Mount for nearly 1,335 years. We're at the end of six thousand years of biblical history, and we're coming up on the two-thousand-year anniversary of the resurrection and ascension. The seventieth Jubilee is at hand. As prophesied, people are traveling like never before, knowledge is exploding, our culture is a mess, and the church in the West is experiencing increasing persecution and apostasy.

Taken together, the ten clues strongly suggest that we are living in the days of Jesus' return.

In other words, Jesus is coming soon. Before long—during the Feast of Trumpets in one of the next few years—the final trumpet is going to sound, the dead in Christ will be raised, those of us who are still alive will be transformed, and we will all be gathered to "meet the Lord in the air." That will begin the sequence of events described in this chapter. When he comes, he will make all of these promises true. And they will be true forever.

Let's look forward with joy and exhilaration to the coming of that day and all the incredible blessings that will follow it. It's going to be amazing—beyond anything we can imagine. And it's just around the corner.

Maranatha. Come soon, Lord Jesus.

THE TEN CLUES

Clue One, Chapter 3 The imminent completion of Jesus' command to "make disciples of every nation." Of twelve thousand people groups—biblical "nations"—on Earth, there are only a few hundred left with no known believers. By God's grace, it is possible that all the remaining groups will hear by the end of 2022.

Clue Two, Chapter 4 The regathering of the nation of Israel. God's Word hints that the generation that sees the nation reborn will live to see the return of Christ. It's now more that seventy years since modern Israel's independence in 1948, so by any reckoning we're getting close to the end of that founding generation.

Clue Three, Chapter 5 The mysterious prophecy from Daniel 12 of the 1,290 days and the 1,335 days, which we interpret to point to the return of Christ in the late 2020s.

Clue Four, Chapter 6 The widely and long-held view that biblical history will have a six-thousand-year span, followed by a thousand-year millennium, echoing the six days of creation and the seventh day of rest. By all accounts we're now at the end of that six-thousand-year period.

Clue Five, Chapter 6 The prophecies of Hosea 5 and 6 that point to a two-thousand-year interval between the departure and the return of the Messiah, followed by a thousand-year period of restoration. Today, the two-thousand-year anniversary of the resurrection and ascension is only a few years away.

Clue Six, Chapter 6 The approaching seventieth Jubilee year in 2025.

Clue Seven, Chapter 7 The condition of our culture. Jesus predicted that the time of his return would be like the days of Noah, which Genesis 6:5 describes like this: "every inclination of the thoughts of the human heart was only evil all the time." Western culture may not be there quite yet, but we're certainly on that path.

Clue Eight, Chapter 7 Paul prophesied that in the last days people would be crying out for "peace and safety." We live in a culture increasingly obsessed with safety and peace.

Clue Nine, Chapter 7 The signs of technology. Daniel 12:4 (NLT) predicts that in the "time of the end . . . many will rush here and there, and knowledge will increase." Could there be a more fitting description of our modern world of jet airplanes and the Internet?

Clue Ten, Chapter 8 The condition of the church. The Bible says that in the last days there will be apostasy and a great falling away in the church—something that we are beginning to see in our day.

The Ten Clues

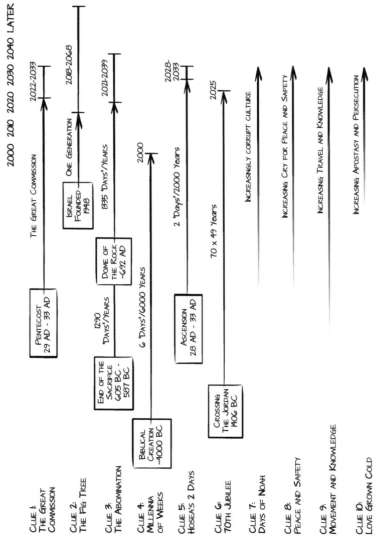

2000 2010 2020 2030 2040 LATER

CLUE 1:
THE GREAT COMMISSION

CLUE 2:
THE FIG TREE

CLUE 3:
THE ABOMINATION

CLUE 4:
MILLENNIA OF WEEKS

CLUE 5:
HOSEA'S 2 DAYS

CLUE 6:
70TH JUBILEE

CLUE 7:
DAYS OF NOAH

CLUE 8:
PEACE AND SAFETY

CLUE 9:
MOVEMENT AND KNOWLEDGE

CLUE 10:
LOVE GROWN COLD

PENTECOST 29 AD - 33 AD
THE GREAT COMMISSION
2022-2033

ISRAEL FOUNDED 1948
ONE GENERATION
2018-2068

END OF THE SACRIFICE 605 BC - 587 BC
1290 "DAYS"/YEARS
DOME OF THE ROCK ~692 AD
1335 "DAYS"/YEARS
2021-2039

BIBLICAL CREATION ~4000 BC
6 "DAYS"/6000 YEARS
2000

CROSSING THE JORDAN 1406 BC
ASCENSION 28 AD - 33 AD
2 "DAYS"/2000 Years
2028-2033

70 x 49 Years
2025

INCREASINGLY CORRUPT CULTURE

INCREASING CRY FOR PEACE AND SAFETY

INCREASING TRAVEL AND KNOWLEDGE

INCREASING APOSTASY AND PERSECUTION

DISCUSSION QUESTIONS

1. What is the most significant or impactful thing you learned from reading this book?
2. Which of the ten clues do you find the most compelling? Why? Do you find any of the clues less convincing?
3. Prophecy can often be confusing and mysterious. Why doesn't God make things clearer? What purpose is served by the mystery?
4. Were you surprised to learn that the church is very close to having preached the good news to all of the world's people groups? Why do you think most American Christians are unaware of the rapidly approaching completion of the Great Commission?
5. God could have accomplished the Great Commission better and faster if he had done the work himself instead of assigning it to us. Why do you think he chose to trust us with that critical work?
6. Ephesians 2:15 says that God's plan is to unite all the world's people groups into one new family under the headship of Christ. How does it make you feel to know that God will one day do away with all racism and hatred between peoples?

7. It's easy to be discouraged by the declining condition of our culture. But it is also easy to get caught up personally in that decline. Are there any ways you are being "conformed to the pattern of this world" as it sinks? What steps might you take to separate yourself from those things?

8. Have you ever experienced persecution as a result of your faith? How does the prospect of facing serious persecution in the coming years make you feel? Do you feel you are prepared for that?

9. It's possible that the antichrist is already on the world scene. Do you have any speculation about who it might be?

10. Does the prospect that Jesus may return in your lifetime excite you? Or are you a little reluctant? Perhaps some of both? Explain why you feel the way you feel. What might increase your excitement about Jesus' return?

11. Do you feel like you're prepared for Jesus' return? If not, what steps will you take to prepare yourself?

12. How do you feel about the idea of eternal rewards? How does the promise of rewards encourage you to seek more ways you can serve and honor God?

13. When you think about heaven, what comes to your mind? What do you imagine it will be like? Do you understand that it will be even better than that?

14. The New Jerusalem will be a place of abundant life. What does the phrase "abundant life" bring to your mind?

15. Having read this book, do you think we can know the season of Jesus' return? How will you respond the next time someone tells you, "You know, Jesus told us that we can't know when he was coming back?"

NOTES

1. Herbert Lockyear, *All the Messianic Prophecies of the Bible* (Grand Rapids, MI: Zondervan, 1973).

2. Alfred Edersheim, *The Life and Time of Jesus the Messiah* (Peabody, MA: Hendrickson Publishers, 1993).

3. Benjamin Blech, "The Miracle of Jewish History," History New Network, Columbian College of Arts & Sciences, The George Washington University, accessed January 21, 2021, http://history newsnetwork.org/article/38887.

4. "Rousseau, Jean Jacques," Encyclopedia.com, accessed January 21, 2021, www.encyclopedia.com/religion/encyclopedias-almanacs -transcripts-and-maps/rousseau-jean-jacquesdeg.

5. Robert Newman, John A. Bloom, and Hugh G. Gauch Jr., "Public Theology and Prophecy Data: Factual Evidence That Counts for the Biblical Worldview," Interdisciplinary Biblical Research Institute, September 2002, www.drjbloom.com/public%20files/PubTheoData .pdf.

6. "Table 2.55, Immigrants by Period of Immigration, Country of Birth, and Last Country of Residence," Statistical Abstract of Israel 2020 No. 71, Israel Central Bureau of Statistics, accessed January 21, 2021, www.cbs.gov.il/en/publications/Pages/2020/Population -Statistical-Abstract-of-Israel-2020-No-71.aspx.

7. Yaron Druckman, "Since 1948, Israel has Welcomed More Than 3 Million New Immigrants," Bridges for Peace, December 17, 2019,

www.bridgesforpeace.com/since-1948-israel-has-welcomed-more
-than-3-million-new-immigrants/.

8. "Vital Statistics: Jewish Population of the World (1882-Present),"
Jewish Virtual Library, accessed January 21, 2021, www.jewish
virtuallibrary.org/jewish-population-of-the-world.

9. "Jewish & Non-Jewish Population of Israel/Palestine (1517-Present),"
Jewish Virtual Library, accessed January 21, 2021, www.jewish
virtuallibrary.org/jewish-population-of-the-world.

10. "World GDP Per Capita Ranking," *The Statistics Times*, August 26,
2020, http://statisticstimes.com/economy/world-gdp-capita-ranking
.php.

11. Stephen H. Futch and Ariel Singerman, "Israel's Dynamic Citrus Industry," *Citrus Industry*, May 7, 2019, https://citrusindustry
.net/2019/05/07/israels-dynamic-citrus-industry/.

12. Gérard Gertoux, "Dating the Reigns of Xerxes and Artaxerxes," *Or-
bis Biblicus et Orientalis Series Archaeologica* 40 (2018): 179–206.

13. Sheila S. Blair, "What Is the Date of the Dome of the Rock," in
BAYT AL-MAQDIS: 'Abd al-Malik's Jerusalem, Part One, ed. Julian
Raby and Jeremy Johns (Oxford: Oxford University Press, 1992),
59–87, https://www.academia.edu/28981754/What_is_the_date
_of_the_Dome_of_the_Rock.

14. Various translations of the inscription are available online, including at www.islamic-awareness.org/history/islam/inscriptions/dotr,
https://ntbc.wordpress.com/inscriptions-about-jesus-on-islams
-dome-of-the-rock-jerusalem/, and in Blair, "What Is the Date of
the Dome of the Rock."

15. Dr. Bob Thiel, "Does God Have a 6,000 Year Plan?," COGwriter.
com, accessed January 21, 2021, www.cogwriter.com/six_thousand
_year_plan_6000.htm.

16. James Barr, "Luther and Biblical Chronology," *Bulletin of the John
Rylands Library* 72, no. 1 (1990): 51–68, www.escholar.manchester
.ac.uk/uk-ac-man-scw:1m2130; James F. McGrath, "Kepler

the Youth-Earth Creationist," Patheos, May 14, 2014, www
.patheos.com/blogs/religionprof/2014/05/kepler-the-young-earth
-creationist.html; "Isaac Newton and Lord Kelvin," The Veritas Forum, January 12, 2016, www.veritas.org/the-age-of-the-earth/.

17. Chuck Missler, "The 7th Millennium: A Calendar Error?," Koino-
nia House, December 1, 1999, https://khouse.org/articles/1999
/183/#notes; Robert Paul Killian, "Jewish Calendar Date Error,"
CrosstheBorder.org, March 6, 2013, https://nicklasarthur.word
press.com/?s=calendar+dat+error; Michael First, *Jewish History in
Conflict: A Study of the Major Discrepancy between Rabbinic and Con-
ventional Chronology* (Northvale, NJ: Jason Aronson, Inc., 1997),
www.google.com/books/edition/Jewish_History_in_Conflict
/9lgZgT73jtEC?hl=en&gbpv=1.

18. Jennifer Warner, "Premarital Sex the Norm in America: Premarital
Sex Research Shows by Age 44, 95% of Americans Have Had Um-
married Sex," WebMD, December 20, 2006, www.webmd.com
/sex-relationships/news/20061220/premarital-sex-the-norm-in
-america.

19. Joseph Chamie, "Premarital Sex: Increasing Worldwide," April 5,
2018, Inter Press Service, April 5, 2018, www.ipsnews.net/2018/04
/premarital-sex-increasing-worldwide/.

20. Greg Lukianoff and Jonathan Haidt, *The Coddling of the American
Mind: How Good Intentions and Bad Ideas Are Setting Up a Generation for Failure* (New York: Penguin Press, 2018), 30.

21. Lily Rothman, "Why Americans Are More Afraid Than They
Used to Be," *Time*, January 6, 1941, https://time.com/4158007
/american-fear-history/.

22. Lukianoff and Haidt, *The Coddling of the American Mind*, 164.

23. Max Roser, "The Spanish Flu (1918-20): The Global Impact of the
Largest Influenza Pandemic in History," Our World in Data, March
4, 2020, https://ourworldindata.org/spanish-flu-largest-influenza
-pandemic-in-history. Roser reports that the 2018 Spanish Flu

killed between 17.4 million and 100 million people worldwide and that the estimated world population in 1918 was 1.8 million.

24. According to Worldometer (www.worldometers.info/world -population/) the world population as of January 14, 2021, was just over 7.8 billion. One percent of 7.8 billion is 78 million; 5.5 percent of 7.8 billion is 429 million.

25. According to Worldometer (www.worldometers.info/coronavirus/), as of January 14, 2021, 2,001,224 people had died from coronavirus worldwide.

26. "President Obama's 2012 Address to U.N. General Assembly (Full Text)," *The Washington Post*, September 25, 2012, www.washington post.com/politics/president-obamas-2012-address-to-un-general -assembly-full-text/2012/09/25/70bc1fce-071d-11e2-afff-d6c7 f20a83bf_story.html.

27. "President Donald J. Trump's Vision for Peace, Prosperity, and a Brighter Future for Israel and the Palestinian People," Global Se-curity.org, accessed January 21, 2021, www.globalsecurity.org /military/library/news/2020/01/mil-200128-whitehouse02.htm

28. Max Roser, "Travel," Our World in Data, accessed January 21, 2021, https://ourworldindata.org/tourism.

29. "Migration," United Nations, accessed January 21, 2021, www.un .org/en/sections/issues-depth/migration/index.html.

30. R. Buckminster Fuller, *Critical Path* (New York: St. Martin's Press, 1981).

31. *World Watch List 2021: The Top 50 Countries Where It Is Most Difficult to Follow Jesus* (Santa Ana, CA: Open Doors, 2021), 3.

32. Rt. Rev. Philip Mounstephen, Bishop of Truro, "Bishop of Truro's Independent Review for the Foreign Secretary of FCO Support for Persecuted Christians: Final Report and Recommendations" (London: Crown, 2019), 16–17, https://christianpersecutionreview.org .uk/storage/2019/07/final-report-and-recommendations.pdf

33. *Persecuted and Forgotten: A Report on Christians Oppressed for their Faith 2015–17 Executive Summary,* Aid to the Church in Need, accessed January 21, 2021, www.churchinneed.org/wp-content /uploads/2017/10/persecution-1-1.pdf.

34. "Nigeria One of the Most Dangerous Countries for Christians, ADF International, December 18, 2020, https://adfinternational .org/news/nigeria-one-of-the-most-dangerous-countries-for -christians/.

35. "The Christians of Iraq and Syria: Debates Over the Nature of Jesus Christ Still Divide His Followers in the Middle East—but Suffering Brings Them Together," *The Economist,* August 4, 2014, www.economist.com/the-economist-explains/2014/08/19/the -christians-of-iraq-and-syria.

36. "Christianity May Disappear from Syria and Iraq—a Call for International Intervention," Religious News Service, October 23, 2019, https://religionnews.com/2019/10/23/christianity-may-disappear -from-syria-and-iraq-a-call-for-international-intervention/.

37. Aaron Keyak, "A Year after Pittsburgh, Anti-Semitism Is Still Rising— and U.S. Jews Blame Trump," Haaretz, October 27, 2019, www .haaretz.com/world-news/.premium-a-year-after-pittsburgh-anti -semitism-is-still-rising-and-u-s-jews-blame-trump-1.8023880.

38. Harriet Sherwood, "Antisemitic Incidents Hit New High in 2019, According to Study: Community Security Trust Recorded 1,805 Incidents, Including a 25% Rise in Violent Assaults," *The Guardian,* February 5, 2020, www.theguardian.com/news/2020 /feb/06/antisemitic-incidents-hit-new-high-in-2019-according -to-study.

39. "German Official Warns Jews against Wearing Kippahs in Public: Anti-Semitic Attacks in Germany Have Surged in the Past Few Years," DW, accessed January 21, 2021, www.dw.com/en/german-official -warns-jews-against-wearing-kippahs-in-public/a-48874433.

40. Luke Baker, "France Shaken by Outbreak of Anti-Semitic Violence and Abuse," Reuters, February 19, 2019, www.reuters.com/article /us-france-antisemitism-protest/france-shaken-by-outbreak-of-anti -semitic-violence-and-abuse-idUSKCN1Q822X.

41. *Cosmos*, episode 1, "The Shores of the Cosmic Ocean," created by Ann Druyan, Carl Sagan, and Steven Soter, directed by Adrian Malone, 1980.

42. Margaret Sanger, *Woman and the New Race* (New York: Truth Publishing Company, 1920), 63.

43. Michael Crichton, "Environmentalism Is a Religion," lecture, The Commonwealth Club, September 15, 2003, San Francisco, www .cs.cmu.edu/~kw/crichton.html.

44. Freeman Dyson, "The Question of Global Warming," *The New York Review*, June 12, 2008, www.nybooks.com/articles/2008/06/12 /the-question-of-global-warming/.

45. Joshua Bote, "He Wrote the Christian Case Against Dating. Now He's Splitting From His Wife and Faith,' Newsweek, July 29, 2019, www.usatoday.com/story/news/nation/2019/07/29/joshua-harris -i-kissed-dating-goodbye-i-am-not-christian/1857934001/

46. Lindsay Elizabeth, "'I'm Genuinely Losing My Faith': Hillsong Worship Leader Rejects Christian Beliefs," CBN News: The Christian Persepctive, August 13, 2019, www1.cbn.com/cbnnews /entertainment/2019/august/im-genuinely-losing-my-faith-hillsong -worship-leader-rejects-christian-beliefs

47. Heather Clark, "Hillsong United Band Leader Calls Jen Hatmaker's Remarks on Homosexuality 'Refreshing'," Christian News, November 5, 2016, https://christiannews.net/2016/11/05/hillsong-united-band-leader-calls-jen-hatmakers-remarks-on-homosexuality -refreshing/

48. David Kinnaman and Gabe Lyons, *unChristian: What A New Generation Really Thinks About Christianity . . . And Why It Matters* (Grand Rapids, MI: Baker, 2012), 44–45.

49. George Barna, *Revolution: Finding Vibrant Faith beyond the Walls of the Sanctuary* (Carol Stream, IL: Tyndale House, 2012), 30–31.

50. George Barna and David Kinnaman, eds., *Churchless: Understanding Today's Unchurched and How to Connect with Them* (Carol Stream, IL: Tyndale Momentum, 2016), 9, 16.

51. Jeffrey M. Jones, *U.S. Church Membership Down Sharply in Past Two Decades*, Gallup, April 18, 2019, https://news.gallup.com /poll/248837/church-membership-down-sharply-past-two-decades .aspx.

52. Drew Dyck, "The Leavers: Young Doubters Exit the Church," *Christianity Today*, November 19, 2010, www.christianitytoday .com/ct/2010/november/27.40.html?start=1.

53. Dyck, "The Leavers."

54. "Most Twentysomethings Put Christianity on the Shelf Following Spiritually Active Teen Years," Barna, September 11, 2006, www .barna.com/research/most-twentysomethings-put-christianity-on -the-shelf-following-spiritually-active-teen-years/.

55. Julia Duin, *Quitting Church: Why the Faithful Are Fleeing and What to Do About It* (Grand Rapids, MI: Baker, 2008), 11, 37.

56. I am indebted to Dr. David R. Reagan of Lamb and Lion Ministries for introducing me to many of the ideas presented in this chapter. You can find his article "The Feasts of Israel: Do They Have Prophetic Significance?" at https://christinprophecy.org/articles/the -feasts-of-israel/.

57. Avi Ben Mordechai, *Signs in the Heavens: A Jewish Messianic Perspective of the Last Days & Coming Millennium* (Millennium 7000 Communications International, 1996), 293–313. For more on the ceremonies surrounding the proclamation of the new moon and the connection between "no one knows the day or the hour" and the Feast of Trumpets, see Chadwick Harvey, "The Mystery of No One Knows the Day or the Hour," http://faithfulperformance.com/the -mystery-of-no-one-knows-the-day-or-the-hour/, and Tony Galli,

"No One Knows the Hour or Day," Hebraic Heritage Ministries International, www.hebroots.org/hebrootsarchive/9807/980715_c .html.

58. Randy Alcorn's books *Money, Possessions, and Eternity* (Wheaton, IL: Tyndale House, 1989) and *The Treasure Principle: Unlocking the Secret of Joyful Giving* (New York: Multnomah, 2001) are excellent surveys of everything the Bible teaches about money and generosity. *Money, Possessions, and Eternity* was an enormous blessing to my wife and me early in our marriage, helping to set us on a path of increasing generosity on which we have remained, by God's grace. I recommend it highly.

59. Again, I recommend Randy Alcorn's *Money, Possessions, and Eternity* and *The Law of Rewards* (Carol Stream, IL: Tyndale House Publishers, 1989) if you'd like to learn more about God's generous promise of eternal rewards for his servants.

THE FINISHING FUND

The Finishing Fund is a partnership of generous Christians who are giving together to send the gospel to the world's last unengaged people groups. Our mission is to accelerate the completion of the Great Commission so that there are "disciples in every nation" by the end of 2022.

In our first three years our partners committed $11.4 million to the Fund, and we supported forty-six projects with twenty-five ministries to engage more than 450 people groups in fifty-one countries with the gospel. The Fund has a minimum investment of $30,000—roughly the cost of a single engagement project. And because the Fund's expenses are covered by its founding partners, 100 percent of each partner's investment goes directly to the field.

For more information, please check out our website at www.finishingfund.org. If you'd like to explore partnership, please email info@finishingfund.org.

ABOUT THE AUTHOR

Douglas Cobb serves as the managing partner of the Finishing Fund, a partnership of kingdom investors who are giving together to accelerate the completion of the Great Commission.

Doug and his wife, Gena, are members of Southeast Christian Church in Louisville, where he teaches the Word by Word Sunday School class and serves as an elder. Gena is a Bible Study Fellowship teaching leader.

Doug is a lifelong entrepreneur. In the past he's served as CEO of Appriss, Greater Louisville Inc., and The Cobb Group; as a managing director with Chrysalis Ventures; and as a director for a variety of companies. He is a three-time *Inc.* 500 CEO and a three-time Kentucky Entrepreneur of the Year.

Doug holds a BA, magna cum laude, from Williams College and an MS in accounting from the New York University Graduate School of Business Administration.

Doug and Gena have been married for forty years and have three grown children and two grandsons.